insight text guide

Anica Boulanger-Mashberg

Like a House on Fire

Cate Kennedy

First published in 2017, reprinted in 2018 (twice), 2019 (twice), 2020,
2021 (twice), 2022, 2023.

Insight Publications Pty Ltd
3/350 Charman Road
Cheltenham VIC 3192
Australia
Tel: +61 3 8571 4950
Fax: +61 3 8571 0257
Email: books@insightpublications.com.au

www.insightpublications.com.au

A catalogue record for this book is available from the National Library of Australia

Cate Kennedy's Like a House on Fire / Anica Boulanger-Mashberg

ISBNs:
9781925485820 (print)
9781925485837 (digital)
9781925485844 (bundle: print + digital)

Cover design by Gisela Beer, based on a concept by The Modern Art Production Group

Printed in Australia by Ligare Book Printers

contents

STORY TABLE

Title	Perspective	Protagonist	Significant other/s*	Central event
Flexion	Third-person limited	Mrs Slovak	Frank Slovak	Frank's accident and recovery
Ashes	Third-person limited	Chris	Chris' mother	Spreading his father's ashes
Laminex and Mirrors	First-person	'the scholar'	(Mr Moreton)	Taking Mr Moreton to the old bathroom
Tender	Third-person limited	Christine	Al	Preparing for a 'lumpectomy'
Like a House on Fire	First-person	Unnamed man	Claire	His back injury; preparing for Christmas
Five-Dollar Family	Third-person limited	Michelle	Jason; Des	Waiting for her milk to come in; having a family portrait taken
Cross-Country	First-person (mostly)	Rebecca	(Her ex)	Stalking her ex online
Sleepers	Third-person limited	Ray	(Sharon)	Attempting to steal some sleepers
Whirlpool	Second-person	Anna	Louise; their parents	Having a family photograph taken
Cake	Third-person limited	Liz	Daniel	Returning to work after maternity leave
White Spirit	First-person	Unnamed woman	(Mandy and Jake)	Completing a community mural
Little Plastic Shipwreck	Third-person limited	Roley	Liz; Samson	The death of a dolphin; Liz's accident
Waiting	First-person	Unnamed woman	Pete	Awaiting a pregnancy scan
Static	Third-person limited	Anthony	Marie; his mother	Family Christmas
Seventy-Two Derwents	First-person	Tyler	Ellie; their mother; Shane; (Mrs Carlyle)	The ongoing threat posed by Shane's presence

* (Secondary or absent characters in brackets)

OVERVIEW

About the author

Cate Kennedy was born in England in 1963 but grew up mainly in Australia. Much of this multi-award-winning writer's work examines contemporary Australian life. Kennedy is perhaps best known for her fiction, including her novel *The World Beneath* (2009), but she has also published a travel memoir and three collections of poetry. *Like a House on Fire* (2012) is Kennedy's second collection of short fiction; the first, *Dark Roots*, was published in 2006. She has won awards for many of her individual poems and stories, as well as having them published independently in numerous Australian and international collections and platforms, including, notably, in the highly competitive and well-respected *New Yorker*. She has also won or been shortlisted for awards for her book-length collections and works. These include the Nita B Kibble Literary Award, the Steele Rudd Award (Queensland Literary Awards), the CJ Dennis Prize for Poetry (Victorian Premier's Literary Awards) and the Stella Prize. These are all honours associated with Australian writing: with presenting Australian life and experience through literature. For example, the Stella Prize is awarded annually to an Australian woman writer of fiction or nonfiction and is named to celebrate the early Australian writer Stella Maria Sarah 'Miles' Franklin (1879–1964), who is known for her contributions to Australian literature.

Like a House on Fire, which won the 2013 Steele Rudd Award, relates urban and rural Australian life without explicitly stating where the stories are set. They are quintessentially Australian, yet they also portray simple human relationships and experiences relevant to other Western cultures. Though some of the vocabulary and settings are specific to Australia, the emotions and ideas within are more broadly human and not solely related to Australian politics, attitudes or experiences.

Kennedy has studied and taught creative writing both in Australia and overseas. She has also edited numerous collections of stories by other writers, such as Black Inc.'s *The Best Australian Stories* (2011), showing her dedication to the form of the short story.

Kennedy lives with her family in Victoria, where she is a regular contributor, speaker and panellist within the literary community, including at writers' festivals and on the radio.

Synopsis

Like a House on Fire comprises fifteen independent short works that each focus on domestic, personal stories. Generally the stories are centred on small crisis points in individuals' lives, such as when they are waiting for medical tests or results, or have just experienced relationship break-ups. Often the crisis points are even smaller: rarely are the stories about life-and-death situations, rather they illustrate miniscule but important emotional challenges such as the conflicts and pressures of Christmas and other family events. The narratives are intimate, domestic close-ups – often composed more of internal reflections and feelings than active events, though most do include key incidents around which the characters' thoughts emerge.

In each of the stories there are the undercurrents of grief, regret, disconnection and imperfection that flow through any human life. Yet at the same time, in most stories there are glimpses of hope, optimism, and resilience, despite all the challenges being faced. In some stories, the positivity is heavily outweighed by the sadness and disappointment, in some there is a closer balance between bleakness and hope, and in others the potential for positive outcomes overrides the sadness. In most cases, however, the stories leave this ultimate evaluation up to the audience, providing evidence both for a reading that emphasises the sadness and one that emphasises resilience in the face of these small human tragedies.

BACKGROUND & CONTEXT

Publication and production history

Many of the stories in *Like a House on Fire* have previously been published individually elsewhere – sometimes more than once – before appearing here together. This is relatively common for single-author collections, and has to do with the nature of the Australian publishing industry. For example, 'Tender' was first published in a multi-author anthology in 2007, five years before this collection. (You can find the list of previous publication credits for the stories on the book's copyright page; this will give you a sense of the range of places the stories have appeared, and the timeframe over which they were written.)

This is worth bearing in mind as you study a collection of short stories. It is a reminder that, although the stories are published as a single volume – and therefore the work itself can be characterised by and discussed in terms of common themes, ideas and even character types – each story does stand alone, and they were composed independently and at different times. This might influence the way you analyse and discuss the collection as a whole.

While it is valid – indeed, important – to consider the themes, ideas and values present in the whole text, it is also worthwhile noting and analysing individual short stories that provide contrasts to the shared features of the whole collection. For example, 'White Spirit' explores a situation beyond the intimate domestic contexts of the other stories; 'Little Plastic Shipwreck' features an animal at the heart of the story, providing a different perspective on human relationships; and 'Whirlpool' is the only story told in the second-person narrative voice. Such differences can provide you with useful points of focus for your exploration and discussion.

Geographical setting

The stories in this collection can all be assumed to take place within Australia, either in rural or urban settings. Some take place indoors (mostly in homes and offices) with little or no reference to the broader geographical environment. Consider how Kennedy communicates the settings, given that the stories rarely mention any landmarks or placenames, and most seem not to be set in specific or 'real' Australian places. Kennedy creates a sense of place in a number of ways, including:

- descriptions of landscapes or urban features (in 'Flexion' and 'Sleepers')
- accounts of the characters' homes (in 'Tender' and 'Whirlpool')
- transitions and journeys within the stories (as in 'Ashes', in which the characters travel to a lake some distance from their home city).

As you read the stories for the first time, try making notes about how setting and location are constructed in each story. You can later draw connections between these settings, their construction, and themes and ideas in the collection.

Historical and social setting

Kennedy's writing is contemporary, set in a social and geographical context that is familiar to many Australian readers. We would describe the content, settings, characters and ideas as 'contemporary' in the sense that they are not of another era, location, culture or reality (as in the alternate realities of speculative fiction or fantasy). However, you will probably notice small details within many of the stories that 'date' the writing, even within only a few years of its 2012 publication. For example, in 'Cross-Country' (first published 2011), the protagonist's internet stalking to track down her ex feels self-conscious, illicit and slightly thrilling in its bravery and scope. This suggests that the capacity to do such stalking was somewhat of a novelty to the character, rather than something that's been around for a number of years. Even the term 'surfing' the web (p.118) is already likely to sound quite dated to many readers. Similarly, at the climax of 'Whirlpool' the photographer is using a film camera rather than a digital camera, and Anna imagines the recipients holding physical prints rather than viewing the photographs on a computer or mobile phone as we might expect to do now. You may like to consider the extent to which even a relatively short time elapsing between composition and reading can affect your interpretation.

GENRE, STRUCTURE & LANGUAGE

Genre

Kennedy is a literary writer (a description that encompasses her fiction, her poetry and even her travel writing), and this collection is no exception, fitting the category of **literary fiction**. Literary writing is work that is judged as having both artistic and social merit. By contrast, genre fiction or popular fiction (such as romance, science fiction or crime fiction) has a greater emphasis on entertainment – although there can be overlaps between genres, and such distinctions are often more useful for commercial (marketing) purposes than for readers' interpretations of a work. However, the genre of a text can provide hints, clues, shortcuts and guidance as to how readers should expect to read and respond to the work.

Genre or popular fiction tends to satisfy a range of conventions, which can include pacing and structure; character types; plot type and plot resolution; settings; and even underlying values. Literary fiction, on the other hand, tends to encompass a broader scope when it comes to generic conventions, and as a genre it does not create specific expectations about these or the writer's other creative decisions. One of the most identifiable elements of literary fiction is its use of heightened and rich language, which may include features such as poetic, descriptive and abstract language; less common narrative perspectives such as the second person ('you'); and distinctive imagery including metaphor and symbolism. (See the 'Language' section for discussion of a number of these features in context.)

At the same time, though, literary fiction may employ very concrete language and construction and use an informal tone and voice – in creating realistic dialogue, for instance. Therefore content can vary distinctly between examples of the genre.

Perhaps the most useful analytical knowledge you can draw from classifying a text as literary fiction relates to the fine-level language use. You can generally assume that, in a piece of literary fiction, language choices at a paragraph and sentence level are very carefully considered, and there are no accidents when it comes to features such as repetition, rhythm, or allusions to other texts or ideas. (Of course, in any text, language choice can be assumed to be highly intentional and careful, but the sentence-level decisions are often less of a priority in genre fiction, for example, where the focus might be pace and plot rather than the construction of poetic rhythm within the prose.) Therefore any of these features that you identify in a literary text can be discussed as significant contributions to the text's meaning.

The other defining genre within which *Like a House on Fire* fits is obviously that of the **short-story collection**. Though it might sound like an obvious descriptor, the definition of 'short story' is somewhat fraught. While the simplest and most concrete characteristic of short stories is their length, this is still not clear-cut: how short (or long) *is* a short story? Formal definitions vary significantly, though individual publishers often have their own word-lengths for various forms. In Australian publishing, a short story is generally understood to be between 1000 and 19000 words. Anything shorter can be placed in other genres, such as flash fiction or micro-fiction, and anything longer is a novel or novella – which is shorter than a novel but longer than a short story. A straightforward guiding principle is that, due to their length, short stories are unlikely to be published alone but rather in literary journals and magazines (which is where many of Kennedy's stories were first published), anthologies (multi-authored collections) or single-author collections like this one.

Characteristics of the genre of short-story *collections* (as opposed to simply short stories) are also wide and varied, though generally there will be a factor or factors that link the stories within a collection. These might be thematic factors; the author's (or authors') cultural, geographical or historical context; a publication context (such as a collection of competition entries); or the particular interests of the editors or publishers. With a single-author text such as *Like a House on Fire*, the obvious factor the stories share is their author, but there are also stylistic and thematic links, and this is why it is worth considering the collection itself as an entity. This is how you can analyse broader ideas, values and concerns and consider recurrent settings, motifs and character types, as well as looking at the differences and similarities across the stories and the ways these divergences and convergences serve to convey narratives and ideas.

Structure

When analysing structure in a text that is a collection, remember that there are two levels to investigate: structure within individual works, and the structure of the collection as a whole. Both can help you to understand and discuss the text.

Structure of individual stories: endings and resolution

The structure of individual stories varies. For example, some begin with the inciting event (like the tractor accident that opens 'Flexion' and therefore the whole collection), while others focus on the lead-up to a key event (as in 'Ashes'). Often this final key event occurs beyond the story's boundaries, as in 'Tender', when we are left guessing at the outcome of Christine's biopsy. Many stories conclude with a glimpse of hope or optimism suggesting that, despite the undercurrents of sadness and struggle in human lives, there is almost always the potential for things to change and, specifically, to improve, even in small ways.

For example, the ending of 'Flexion' offers a hint that the accident may have brought about a change in the dynamic of the Slovaks' relationship, as Frank's wife recognises her husband's vulnerability, and chooses to respond to it with quiet, gentle compassion and even love (as suggested by the word 'heart' in the final sentence, p.16). Another example is the ending of 'Laminex and Mirrors', where the final paragraph is full of song, laughter and pleasure, and the protagonist is 'content ... to believe ... that this path before us will stretch on forever' (p.56). Here the content of the story offers a striking contrast with the structure, as the final words speak of an eternal experience while their position in the story provides a clear suggestion of finality (as the little excursion has likely cost the protagonist her job) and even mortality (for Mr Moreton).

Structure of the collection: contrasts and themes

One of the most important structural elements in a collection is the order in which the stories are presented to readers. Sometimes works are ordered chronologically, based on when the author wrote them (more common for posthumous collections), but more frequently the publisher or editor has selected an order that best suits the works. In this collection, the themes and tones are fairly consistent throughout, so other key factors such as the age or narrative perspective of the protagonist have been varied to keep readers' interest by offering contrast between the stories. Consider how this impacts on your understanding of key themes.

For example, had the stories been arranged to progress from those featuring younger characters to those featuring older characters, we could comment on how the collection as a whole presents a view of human lifespans, transitions and ageing. As it is, we can argue that Kennedy wants to present her themes as universal rather than as age-dependent human experiences. In fact, the final story features a young narrator, suggesting that the small tragedies in life are not restricted to any one age or period; they are an essential part of human existence. Note that the ending of this final story contains optimism, thus lending the whole collection a positive tone, despite containing much evidence to the contrary.

Language

While the text is frequently poetic and descriptive, at the same time the language is often sparse and simple. The length of the stories provides some indication of this: although each story contains strong imagery and figurative language, the longest is less than forty pages (and the text is well-spaced throughout, with pages averaging only around 250 words) with the others all around fifteen or twenty pages. This indicates that Kennedy uses concise, efficient language to communicate each story.

Repetition and language-play

Kennedy frequently uses repetition of words, phrases and imagery within stories, helping to generate cohesion as well as to emphasise important ideas, images and themes. For example, in 'Cross-Country' the phrase 'high lonesome sound' is used to describe both the music the couple once heard (p.121) and her ex's imagined voice (p.125); each use emphasises the story's exploration of the idea of loneliness and what it can make people do. By using the phrase more than once, Kennedy draws our attention to it and creates connections between the associated ideas, here linking the past (the music) with the present (the absence of the ex).

Kennedy plays with language in a number of other ways, including, notably, in the stories' titles, which often carry multiple meanings, as with 'Sleepers', 'Waiting', 'Static', 'Tender' and 'Whirlpool'. Consider the word 'static', for example, which, in the story of that name, has the literal meaning of static (crackling noises) on the walkie-talkies, but also the figurative 'static' (atmospheric disturbance) that exists between Anthony and his family, as well as between Anthony and Marie, interfering with clear communications. There is also a third connotation, as the title points us towards a distinct motif of the story: static in the sense of standing still. Anthony's life seems to be in a sort of holding pattern, where the same conflicts and disconnections recur and he doesn't know how to escape. As you study each of the stories, remember to look for clues about meaning, themes and ideas within the titles.

Figurative language

Descriptive, rich language is a characteristic of this collection, even while it often describes mundane, simple, everyday experiences, relationships and moments. Remember that Kennedy is also a published poet, so it is not surprising that her use of language is careful, lyrical and concise even when she is writing prose. Below is an example of a descriptive passage from one of the stories, with a brief analysis of the techniques used.

Consider the following sentence from 'Waiting':

> This careful professional detachment while they're gazing at the human map of you, the intimate, failed, faltering misstep, in ghostly black and white. (p.213)

Some of the language techniques used in just this one sentence include the following:

- metaphor (a person as a map)
- alliteration ('**f**ailed, **f**altering') as well as assonance ('hu**m**an **m**ap ... inti**m**ate')
- personification (describing a medical condition as a 'misstep')
- descriptive figurative language (emotive and poetic words such as 'gazing', 'faltering', 'ghostly')
- concrete description including allusion to senses ('black and white')
- second-person perspective ('you') – a less common perspective that puts the reader in the protagonist's position, increasing audience connection and engagement.

The subsequent sentence extends the metaphor of the human as a map, expanding it into a broader analogy of the scan as a landscape: 'white cloud coursing grainily over a black landmass, some cyclone gathering its bleary force offshore' (p.213). Again the language is poetic and descriptive, using the weather as a metaphor for the protagonist's 'gathering' emotion.

Symbolism

The cover of the Scribe edition (designed by Allison Colpoys) uses simple visual symbolism the way Kennedy uses symbolism in language, and it perfectly encapsulates the miniscule griefs and sorrows of the domestic stories. The household objects represented are all familiar, mundane symbols of domesticity, and most carry connotations of comfort, beauty and pleasure: flowers, jewellery, a teacup, wine. Yet on closer inspection each of these objects (with the possible exception of the doily forming the 'o' in 'House', and the chicken on the book's spine) is somehow damaged or distorted: the picture frame is empty, the flowers in the vase are drooping and losing their petals, the cup of tea is spilled, the tap dripping, the necklace broken, the iron unplugged. The associations are of domestic bliss shattered, of objects unable to fulfil their potential. At the same time, however, many of the objects do not seem destroyed beyond repair: the smashed plate looks as if all its parts are there, available to be glued back together; the dirty single socks could be washed.

These ideas resonate with the themes and tones of the short stories within: while personal tragedies permeate nearly all the stories, most contain or conclude with glimpses of hope, of the possibility of better futures. Often when Kennedy uses figurative language, motifs or images, symbolism and analogy in her stories, they perform a similar role to these images on the cover, helping us to visualise the ideas and themes.

STORY-BY-STORY ANALYSIS

Flexion (pp.1–16)

Summary: *Frank Slovak survives a serious tractor accident on his farm. His wife cares for him as he makes a slow, stubborn recovery. Gradually they both accept their new reality of his limitations and dependence on her.*

This first story in *Like a House on Fire* introduces many of the recurring themes, ideas, motifs and character types within the collection. It also inducts readers immediately into the emotional tone that permeates the collection. For example, disconnection and sadness between partners is a recurring relationship style in many of the stories.

In this first story, the marital relationship between the Slovaks is strained at best, becoming more uncomfortable with the impact of the tragedy of Frank's accident, which forces him to become dependent on her in a practical sense. He is resentful and, at first, so is she: she feels 'cheated' when he does not die from pneumonia during his initial hospital stay (p.6). But gradually she finds strength and agency in her position as a carer – a strength she was denied in their past, for instance when Frank dictated their emotional journey following the loss of their unborn child – and this slight shift in power in their relationship, while challenging, is not unwelcome to her. When she insists he swallow his pride, anger and sullenness to thank those who have helped him in his recovery, she feels 'exhilaration' (p.13) at being able to force him into an action he is resisting.

This small, rare victory for her seems to prompt miniscule, cautious expressions of affection between them: Frank's admission that dying at the scene of the accident would have been the one kindness he could have afforded her (p.15), and her active compassion in the act of reaching out to hold his hand as they lie in bed (pp.15–16). Despite 'hating him' (p.8) and feeling a 'pure' 'loathing' (p.10), she finds herself 'determinedly' (p.16) reaching out to help ease his suffering. The story ends with this image of a small hope in a landscape of bleak acceptance as they face a difficult future together.

The sense of delicate optimism concluding this story is also a hint of what is to come in the collection: while the stories are full of desperation, in many cases the characters find reason to carry on, despite – and sometimes even because of – their circumstances and the terrible events that have befallen them.

Key point

Consider the impact of narrative voice: because we have access to Mrs Slovak's internal perspective, it is easier for readers to empathise with her than with the irritable Frank, even at times when she is 'daydreaming' (p.7) of the benefits she might reap from his injury and incapacity. Normally this would seem a behaviour that might alienate audiences from a character, but the limited third-person perspective gives us insight into *why* she might feel this way, and helps us see the situation from her side.

Q Why do you think this story has been chosen as the first in the collection?

Q Read the paragraph beginning 'She instantly sees the mobile phone' (p.2), where Mrs Slovak observes the emotions her trapped husband is experiencing. How do Kennedy's language choices in this paragraph compare with those in the rest of the story? How does this influence the reader so early in the piece?

Ashes (pp.17–33)

Summary: *Chris reluctantly accompanies his mother on a trip to scatter his father's ashes in a lake where the young Chris went fishing with his father. His relationship with his mother is a focus, as she puts various emotional pressures on him during their trip. Their interactions are interwoven with Chris' memories of his growing up and relationship with his parents.*

Carrying on from the sense of strained relationships established in 'Flexion', 'Ashes' takes up a similar tone and explores the frustrations and patterns of tension that can exist between two people who are closely tied together. This time, the two central characters are not a married couple but a mother and son (though Chris' relationship with his father is also a significant thread in the story, as are his recollections of his relationship with his ex, Scott). In 'Ashes', as in the first story, years of habit and history underlie the imperfect relationship between the two central characters. Though Chris begins with good intentions of satisfying his mother's emotional needs and fulfilling her insistent desire to reconstruct a past that was never quite real, part way through the first sentence of the story as they embark on what he calls a *'pitiful pilgrimage'* (p.27), he 'is already feeling his staunch goodwill leaking away' (p.17).

Again in this story, the readers' sympathies and empathy lie most easily with the character with whom the narrative voice is aligned (Chris). This is not because this character is portrayed as flawless. Rather, as with Mrs Slovak, we are able to see things from Chris' perspective and are naturally encouraged to understand the pressures he is under, while the behaviour of the other character (here his mother) is shown to be hurtful – for example, she aggressively rejects his attempts to offer an alternative to her worries about leaving the ashes in the car (p.20). Far from being insensitive, Chris reveals his awareness of his own imperfections and contributions to familial tensions, acknowledging, for instance, that his mother is 'grieving … vulnerable' yet he 'can't help' feeling intolerant and judging her (p.23).

By constructing a central character with such honesty about his own limitations, Kennedy encourages readers to trust his perspective and to empathise with his journey, which is one of grieving – as his mother's is too, but in a different way. This is another recurrent dynamic throughout the collection: characters who share a situation or challenge but have such different experiences or approaches that they are unable to find much comfort in each other. Here, although Chris and his mother share a lifetime, she recalls 'happy memories of all those fishing trips' (p.23) while his perspective differs; there were really only two such trips – neither enjoyable – and he can only remember that past as yet another of the 'powerless indignities of childhood' (p.23). Shared history does not equate to shared reality. For Chris, the 'embellished past' (p.26) that his mother clings to is yet more evidence of his family's inability to recognise reality for what it truly is – demonstrated by his parents' refusal to accept his homosexuality.

As the story concludes, the ashes become a tidy symbol for what has become of all Chris' regrets and sadness about his past and his relationship with his parents. The ashes are an innocuous yet sad 'drift of grey and white particles' and 'he can't believe this is all that's left' (p.32) – not just of his father but, the tone implies, of a shared past, flawed as it was, and also of the story itself as the imagery becomes self-reflexive, signposting the structure of the narrative. In the final moments, the traumatic occasion triggers a small gesture of human connection between the two seemingly irreconcilable characters, as Chris 'tenderly' and caringly dusts the small smear of ash off his mother's jacket (p.33). As with the first story, from the sadness and difficulty emerges a tiny symbol of hope, kindness, and even connection between the two that is so painfully lacking throughout.

Q Which moment in this story stands out most clearly in your mind after your first reading? Why? Go back and re-read that section of the story and look carefully at the text to see which elements of narrative structure, language choice, imagery, character development or other features might have made that moment so memorable.

Laminex and Mirrors (pp.35–56)

Summary: *The unnamed central character works as a cleaner in a hospital to save money for an overseas trip. She doesn't fit in easily with the other staff, but is kind to them (even buying jewellery and cosmetics she does not want, solely to help the seller earn a sought-after bonus Christmas gift). She befriends one of the elderly hospital patients, Mr Moreton, risking her job in order to treat him to a bath in an about-to-be-demolished bathroom, and to an illicit cigarette in a courtyard.*

The protagonist, nicknamed 'the scholar' by her hospital workmates because hers is a more intellectual background than theirs (she puzzles them by reading a book for enjoyment), has just finished school and is saving for an overseas trip. She is embarking on grand personal adventures at the beginning of her life, optimistic and, as she describes it, 'eager-beavering' her way towards her future (p.35). In strong contrast, Mr Moreton is at the other end of his life, and knows he is soon to die. Yet the two form a gentle connection, based on little but their both being in the same place, passing the days until they will 'leave' the hospital, one way or another.

'Laminex and Mirrors' differs from the first two stories in that it is less infused with grief, and more with a sense of hope, despite the fact that one of the central characters is dying. The hospital setting subtly reflects the difference between the young character at the beginning of a journey and the older character at the end of one, in an illustration of how setting can symbolise themes and content. The hospital is being upgraded for its own shiny new journey, 'every wing' soon to have 'glistening white ensuite bathrooms and upmarket floral bedspreads' (p.39). But at the same time there is an 'ancient' bathroom 'slated for demolition' (p.39) – which the protagonist is sent to clean as punishment for being friendly with the patients, and specifically with Mr Moreton. However, she turns the punishment to a positive (just as small gestures of hope and affection emerge from the tragedies and struggles in other stories), taking Mr Moreton to enjoy a treat of having a bath and, subsequently, smoking a cigarette he has begged her for. As with the hard-earned cash she hands over to help Dot reach her cosmetics sales goal, 'the scholar' willingly sacrifices her own job security to bring some joy to an old man.

Q How does this story differ from the first two? In what ways are they similar?

Tender (pp.57–72)

Summary: *Christine prepares dinner and the next day's lunches for her family the night before a biopsy on a lump in her breast. She then helps her young son with a last-minute homework project, finishing it for him overnight.*

This story offers a gentle glimpse into the daily life and emotions of a family of four, focused through the mother, Christine, and her fears about her upcoming 'lumpectomy' (p.58). This key event (which takes place outside the timeframe of the story) crystallises the dynamics of the relationships in the family – particularly that between Christine and Al. It prompts for Christine to ponder her family life and her partner's character, described as frustratingly 'vague' (p.63) and 'distracted' (p.64), but also as 'laid-back ... amiable' (p.63), depending on how Christine is feeling. While the story reveals her frustration at how much work she puts in to keeping the family running (work Al seems unaware of), there is little tension evident in their relationship; rather they are portrayed as gently, comfortably happy together, despite the incompleteness of their house and the daily mundane challenges and nuisance of keeping their life on track. This provides a contrast with many of the other stories in the collection, where couples manage to maintain relationships, but experience the long-term sorrows of disconnection, lack of love or incompatibility.

Key point

This story may seem to skate over the surface of deeper issues – such as the possibility of Christine having cancer – but in fact acknowledges these issues through subtle symbolism. For example, when Christine 'keeps recalling Al, suddenly surprising her by shaking those pyjamas right-way-out with that one deft easy motion' (p.71), and feels comforted, she 'can't think why' (p.71). This simple moment has somehow symbolised for her that if the worst happened and she did not survive, Al would be able to cope and to care for the children, despite his sometimes hopeless-seeming, casual attitude.

The lump, with its implied possibility of cancer, symbolises a kind of wake-up call from an idealism that characterises Christine and Al's past. The never-quite-completed house that they built and the herbal and alternative medicines languishing in the pantry (p.62) similarly represent a 'grand theory of sustainability modified to a more prosaic reality' (p.59). Although there is little indication one way or the other about the likely outcome of the biopsy (which is not the point of the story), structurally the narrative could indicate that this moment in time is a turning point in the family's life – the last time they knew the world before a cancer diagnosis – simply because this is the moment the story reveals to us. This interpretation is justifiable, when looking at how the structure conveys meaning, but note that it is only one possible interpretation and others are justified too.

For example, as Christine finishes her son's homework for him (creating a 'perfect … little microcosmic landscape', or representation of the world in a diorama, p.71), the tone of the story becomes optimistic, as reflected in the language choices. The sun rises (a common symbol for hope and renewal), making the landscape outside look 'defiant … like a healing scar' (p.71), and as Christine releases the mousetraps, literally releasing tension, they settle very reassuringly 'with a benign and harmless snap' (p.72). The choice of the word 'benign' – commonly associated with harmless tumours – is very deliberate, and counteracts Christine's earlier fearful repetition of its opposite, *'Malignant. Malignant.'* (p.64). These language features provide strong support for an interpretation of the story as suggesting that Christine's outcome will be positive.

Key vocabulary

Malignant or benign: the words are not exclusively medical terms and in general usage mean, respectively, dangerous or inclined to cause distress, and kind or favourable. However, they are commonly used in association with tumour diagnosis, respectively meaning cancerous or invasive, and harmless or non-cancerous.

Q What evidence does the story give that Christine's and Al's lives have drifted from their ideals? What tone does Kennedy use to communicate this?

Like a House on Fire (pp.73–93)

Summary: *A father with a spinal injury tries to force his three children to enjoy putting up the family Christmas tree, while his wife is at work. As Christmas approaches his recovery is slower than expected, raising concerns the condition may be psychosomatic.*

In the eponymous story (the story with the same title as the collection), two tensions are apparent almost immediately. One is in the central relationship (between Claire and her husband, the unnamed protagonist). The other is more thematic: a tension between the normally celebratory time of year (Christmas) and the sorrowful, difficult atmosphere in the family as the protagonist struggles with his injury and with the long-term unemployment and physical and psychological pain his incapacitation causes him. He feels 'like a beaten dog' (p.77) and is all too aware of the strain his injury is putting on the family.

These tensions gain significance as the story progresses, through a series of key word choices and images.

- The father drops and smashes the Christmas decorations (p.74), symbolising the damage his injury has done to what should be a time of family celebration.
- The choice of the words 'kill the occasion' and 'poisoned it' (p.77) show the extremes of the damage he feels he is doing, and of his suffering.
- Kennedy uses vivid imagery of the man's physical injury to describe the conflict in the relationship: the couple's communication has been reduced to 'the tiny squeezed and inflamed gap' that is the injured space in his spinal disc (p.79).

The 'immobilising pain' (p.82) of the protagonist infects all the characters. Even the youngest child in the story – four-year-old Evie, who should be full of the innocent pleasures of childhood – is described with eyes 'that are all too familiar with endlessly compromised plans, as if life is already revealing itself to her as a long trail of small disappointments' (p.76). This description tells us as much about her father, the narrator and protagonist, as it does about her. He is primed to see sadness in his world, and to recognise (or possibly misdiagnose or at least exaggerate) it in others.

Key point

The symbolism underlying the title of this story (and of the collection) is explored by the narrator as he considers the meaning of the cliché. He notes that it perfectly captures his experience. His reflections also capture one of the collection's central themes: the idea that small tensions, conflicts and sadnesses can hold the power to overwhelm entire minds, relationships and families, just as flames can overcome a house: 'flickering small resentments licking their way up into the wall cavities ... everything threatening to go roaring out of control' (pp.86–7).

Key vocabulary

Psychosomatic: (from *psyche*, relating to 'mind' and *soma*, relating to 'body') refers to physical disorders or symptoms that cannot be explained medically, and instead are attributed to mental or emotional influences. The word is often used in a derogatory way, to discredit someone's experience, but psychosomatic does not actually mean 'faked'.

Q Why do you think this story has been chosen as the one to give the collection its name?

Five-Dollar Family (pp.95–113)

Summary: *A new young mother struggles with feeding her baby. Discovering that her unfaithful partner, the baby's father, is going to court and likely to be imprisoned, she urgently tries to arrange a family photo session in the mall – even though the doctors consider her unready to leave the hospital.*

In another story of distance between people, and relationships dominated by sadness, Michelle tries to construct for herself, even if only temporarily, a moment of 'happy families' that she might one day look back on for comfort. As with the previous story, this one is set around an event traditionally associated with joy, hope, excitement and pleasure. While of course the realities of childbirth and new parenthood are also filled with challenge and struggle, positive symbolism commonly associated with birth and babyhood include:

- innocence and the idea of a new life as a 'clean slate'
- joy, celebration and the love shared by a growing family
- good fortune (children are often thought to be a blessing, and can also bring practical wealth and strength to a family).

The events of 'Five-Dollar Family' undermine these associations, again constructing narrative tensions between familiar cultural symbols and the reality of individual situations. The clean slate is almost immediately marred by Michelle's knowledge that Des will probably not come home from his 'court thing' (p.107); this also indicates that they are unlikely to be celebrating their new life together as a family. Rather than heralding good fortune, Jason's birth comes in a week when his father is likely to face jail. Further, the appeal of the bargain price put on 'family' by the discount photographer reminds us that Michelle is not blessed with wealth along with her new child. In fact she is upset when Des spends too many of their limited dollars on a ridiculous jacket for Jason, when she 'hasn't even got a change table' (p.109).

Yet, as in other stories in the collection, the dismantling of illusory expectations (for instance, Michelle's 'vague idea' that when the baby was born, Des would become some sort of greeting-card cliché of a loving father, p.102) is accompanied by the empowerment of a new reality. For example, Michelle is deeply overwhelmed with the responsibility of caring for her new baby and, before the birth, had hoped her hapless boyfriend Des would step up to be strong and to care for the family. When he does not, she begins to find new strength in herself, recognising that 'she's got everything this baby needs, now' (p.113). She does not have to rely on a weak, unsupportive and unfaithful partner.

The final paragraphs, however, are equivocal. While Michelle embraces her new capability to care for her child, the moment carries an unsettling mood which is likened to 'a shiver rippling out of your control' (p.113). We are reminded that triumph and grieving are often closely linked.

Q Michelle's determination to have the family photographed shows her strength. What else does it tell you about her as a character?

Cross-Country (pp.115–26)

Summary: *Rebecca struggles to recover after a break-up: staying away from work and stalking her ex online. Seeing his name on a running-club's website, she plans to take up running herself, for the joy of overtaking him in a race then casually ignoring him afterwards. After considering this for many days, she realises the listed person can't be him (it is an under-fourteens results list) and the story ends as she symbolically closes her computer.*

The sadness and disconnection in this story is explicit whereas in many other stories it is an undertone, subtext or mood. Here, Rebecca actively struggles with the loss of her relationship. Both angry and grieving, she is unable to return to her work or normal life. She spends her energy trying to track her ex online, hoping at first just to find some trace of him, since he has excised himself so fully from her life. She tracks 'his' results on a running-club website, constructing an elaborate plan for a gentle sort of revenge against him, before realising it isn't him she's found online but a kid with the same name. This realisation closes a door (or 'windows', as she puns in the final paragraph) on a chapter of her life, as she gives up on finding him, realising that 'it's time to roll the credits' (p.126). This, along with the phone call from her boss (an intrusion into her fantasy life) suggests that she will move on to a new phase – whether better or worse is left unclear, but the narrative hints that she will find a way to move on.

Key point

There is a shift in narrative point of view in this story, which begins in the second person ('you'): an unusual perspective. This has the effect of immediately forcing readers to make a more personal connection than they might otherwise have had, putting them in the position of the story's protagonist. (See 'Whirlpool' for a story that uses the second person for the whole narrative.)

Q Why do you think Kennedy begins the story in the second person but then shifts to first person?

Q Do you think Rebecca knew all along that the runner she was stalking online was not her ex? Why or why not? How do the language choices and narrative structure lead you to your conclusion?

Sleepers (pp.127–39)

Summary: *Ray, 'not exactly unemployed' (p.134), finds himself in a kind of stasis after his break-up, lacking motivation or energy to do much with his life. When he decides to follow others in the town and pilfer some railway sleepers that are being pulled up and sorted for disposal, he is caught by the police.*

This story offers yet another portrait of the emotional distance and damage between two people. Ray's early description of Sharon, his ex (before she was his ex), notes her 'mouth a sour twist' and his feeling in response to her of 'something creeping over him like a slow anaesthetic' (p.128). This is one of the story's numerous images of stagnancy, inaction or 'deep dragging inertia' (p.128). The title sums this up, as well as referring to the central concrete event with the railway sleepers: Ray has become a 'sleeper' in his own life. There is the suggestion that such stagnancy may have been what pushed Sharon to leave him, as in her weary exasperation at his lack of motivation to do any landscaping at their rental property.

Other instances of imagery and language that reiterate the theme of slowness include the following.

- When the story opens, Ray is stuck in traffic, a form of inactivity in itself, and he feels himself 'lapsing into' a 'lethargic kind of trance' (p.127).
- At the traffic lights 'he idled' (p.129) – this describes the literal action of his car, but is another example of the regular use of language relating to the theme.
- The signs in the roadworks – *'SLOW. SLOW. STOP.'* symbolise his emotional state (p.129).
- He is so static that he can even wake up in the morning 'with an empty plate from last night still sitting on his chest ... in exactly the same position' as when he went to sleep (p.132).
- Ray thinks there might be something physically wrong with him, justifying the 'bottomed-out energy, the sapped, exhausted feeling' compared to others' 'focus' (p.132) and when he tries to converse at the barbeque, he comes up with 'nothing' (p.133).
- He again finds himself in the car 'at the crossing, sitting motionless' (p.137) – both the crossing and the lack of motion are symbolic of where he is at in his life.
- He 'kept finding himself ... eyes closed like he was hibernating' and had to 'rouse himself to move' (p.138).
- The wood of the sleepers represents the protagonist: 'so much life in it, still, it just broke your heart to see it go to waste' (p.139).

Such symbols recur throughout the collection (including in story titles such as 'Waiting' and Static') but are most prominent in this story.

When at last Ray stirs himself out of his emotional stupor and takes action – taking some of the sleepers, partly to do something nice for Sharon and prove himself to her, but also for himself – he is punished by being caught by the police, despite so many others in the town having already got away with it. The story leaves him there, trapped once again in his own life, waiting patiently to 'take what was coming to him' (p.139). The ending suggests that he has no hope of change.

Q Compare the ending of this story with that of the previous one. Both stories feature single characters struggling post–break-up. How do the endings differ? How does this influence your understanding of each story's meaning?

Whirlpool (pp.141–53)

Summary: *Pre-teen Anna longs to escape to the family's above-ground pool, which her mother scorns (not least because it is associated with Anna's father, also an object of her mother's scorn). Her mother insists on a professional family photo to send out with Christmas cards. The event highlights the tensions running under the surface for the family, not unlike the currents of the kids' swimming-pool whirlpools.*

The protagonist in this story is younger than any others so far, offering a contrast to the perspectives in the first half of the book and foreshadowing the final and longest story in the collection. Again there is a focus on the vast distance and lack of love within a couple. This distance is illustrated poignantly by the family photos where Louise and Anna's father is literally only a shadow, having been behind the camera, taking the photo – yet their mother still refers to 'all' of them in the image, as though she barely notices his absence (p.142). The same emotional distance is echoed between the daughters, who 'silently' decorate the Christmas tree in summer, diligent and obedient but 'ignoring each other' (p.143). This recalls the forced celebration tradition of tree-decorating in the titular story as again Kennedy contrasts supposedly happy times – summer and Christmas – with emotional disquiet. Only in the pool do the sisters 'break' their 'pattern of avoidance' (p.145) to create whirlpools. Here the girls influence their physical environment powerfully, in a way they are unable to emotionally as children in a household with unhappy parents, particularly a mother who tries to drag them onto her side of any conflict.

The professional family photograph is the ultimate symbol of denial of the tensions and conflicts in the family – the parents' lack of connection, the petty sibling cruelties, the mother's inability to understand her daughters' needs. Yet, as in so many of the stories, this painful symbol of disconnection also prompts one of the few moments of genuine optimism: Louise and Anna spontaneously and briefly unite for a moment against their mother, not smiling in the photograph. This echoes the significant moments surrounding family photographs in 'Five-Dollar Family' and 'Static'.

Key point

The overseas friends to whom the mother will send Christmas cards (p.148) are a symbol of her insistence on keeping up appearances. They recall the Book Club Women from 'Ashes': acquaintances for whom these women feel a need to maintain a pretence of some sort of happy family, despite the imperfections and disjunctions that are the reality.

Q What do you think Anna means when she says, 'the sundresses are about your mother' (p.152)?

Cake (pp.155–79)

Summary: *Liz leaves her toddler Daniel at day care on her first day back at work after maternity leave, then struggles to get through the workday as her colleagues take her out to lunch, and she plods through a tedious meeting before being able to leave work and collect Daniel to go home. She ends by breaking her resolution about no longer breastfeeding him.*

The idea of distance between people recurs in this story. The other mothers at work feel quite differently about their parenting experiences and obligations, creating a real chasm in their relationships with Liz. However, one of the greatest distances is between Liz and her baby son. This distance, unlike so many others in the collection, is not one of lost connection, emotional incompatibility or conflict. Rather, the physical distance – enforced by Liz needing to return to work – is what creates the emotional distance, and Liz 'craves' the 'weight' of holding her son (p.166), as she struggles to get through her first day back at work without him. In this way, the painful interpersonal gap still thematically reflects those in other stories, but has a quite different cause and background. It is painful because of the strength of love, rather than its absence or disappearance.

Q How would you describe the tone of the workplace scenes? And the final scene as Liz feeds Daniel? How does Kennedy create these different moods?

White Spirit (pp.181–95)

Summary: *A woman co-ordinates a mural being painted in a multicultural estate's community centre. The painters aim for ethnic authenticity in their representations, while the community itself remains uninterested. The mural is launched and is an official success, acquitting its grant aims, despite evidence that members of the local community do not care much about it.*

This story's setting and context are unusual in the collection, as it takes place in a public rather than a domestic space and the central conflicts and concerns are not those of a family or a couple. However, the difference is subtle, as the story's focus remains on the personal rather than professional world of a residential community (much like an extension of family). In this sense, its concerns align with those elsewhere in the collection.

The community in 'White Spirit' echoes the disjointedness and disappointments of couples and families in other stories. The chasm between ideal and reality results in a deflated sadness, primarily for the unnamed protagonist, who experiences unmet expectations, but also to some extent for the painters Mandy and Jake and some of the residents of the multicultural estate. The only characters who are not let down are those who are so removed as to not recognise the reality, such as the 'thrilled' centre director (p.188) or the minister who attends the opening. They see only the 'authentic ethnic food', the 'grassroots community development', and a 'positive message', interpreting the mural and the event as a complete success (p.192), when in fact the protagonist has revealed how superficial this success is. She has had to bribe the community to be involved in the mural, but the symbolic coating with an impervious sealant prevents any real input from the community, marking the multicultural representation as a true act of the 'white spirit'. Here the title alludes to the racial diversity of the estate yet also to the (implied) 'whiteness' of its administrators and supporters.

Key point

Like many stories in the collection, 'White Spirit' concludes on a note of optimism: despite the vast chasms present in the narrative (between ideal and reality; between cultures; between individuals), the final moments feature an image of closeness, as the protagonist says, 'I feel two arms on either side of me, stretching tentatively round my waist, drawing me tighter' and the final image is of her 'smile' (p.195). Thus the story leaves readers with positives that counter the bleak disillusionment throughout.

Q Think about the title of this story. How many literal (concrete) and figurative (symbolic) meanings can you come up with? How do these ideas help you understand the story?

Little Plastic Shipwreck (pp.197–209)

Summary: *Roley, an employee of Oceanworld, discovers that Samson, the sole remaining dolphin at the theme park, has died. Having cared for Samson, he refuses to 'freeze it and cut it up' (p.207) as ordered, and consequently loses his job, returning home to his wife Liz who has recovered physically but not psychologically from a severe accident.*

Oceanworld, a 'sad cluster of concrete pools and enclosures surrounded on all sides by murals depicting a far bigger, shinier aquatic adventure park' (p.198), is a clear illustration of the gap between idealism and reality. Like the mural in 'White Spirit' that tells a shiny lie to its audience, the theme park appeals to what people would prefer reality to be.

The animals at Oceanworld echo the kinds of emptiness and entrapment in their worlds that the humans in other stories portray: Rex the sea-lion does nothing but 'compulsively' repeat motions in his enclosure; the turtles are 'totally vacant'; the penguins are 'shifty'; and 'of course the fish had no expression whatsoever' (p.202). It is no accident the story opens with the death of Samson, 'the only creature at the aquarium … able to create a facial expression' (p.201), a creature Roley describes as 'loving' (p.201), 'sensitive' (p.207) and 'full of such understanding, and such forgiveness' (p.208). Symbolically, his death represents the removal of love, sensitivity and understanding from Roley's world. In his home life, Roley is coping with being a carer for his wife Liz, who was in an induced coma after a serious accident.

Just as Samson symbolises what is hopeful and positive in Roley's life, so the rest of the animals echo the emptiness in his relationship with Liz, who has physically recovered but is a listless, puzzled shell of her former self. Indeed, she now has a 'permanently quizzical expression' (p.208) and an 'emptied, passive face' (p.209) just like the blank-faced animals at Oceanworld. This empty bleakness is stronger in this story than others, as it is not mediated by any glimmer of hope in the story's conclusion. Rather, Samson is dead, Roley is unemployed, and Liz shows no sign of ever recovering her emotional and personal life.

Q Re-read the paragraph on page 202 about the fish, from which this story takes its name. How does Kennedy use the idea of the fish to illustrate themes in this story? How does this illuminate the collection as a whole?

Waiting (pp.211–18)

Summary: *A woman visits a hospital alone for a scan in early pregnancy. She reflects on her previous miscarriages and on her partner's anticipation and his hopes both for a child and a successful wheat crop. The story concludes before she goes in for her test.*

As in a number of the other stories, the title has multiple meanings and connotations. The woman is literally in a hospital waiting room, waiting for her procedure (and anticipates sitting there again afterwards, waiting for the result). But in a broader sense she is waiting for something in her life to change – waiting to have a successful pregnancy and family, waiting for her hopes to be fulfilled. Her partner Pete is waiting for these things too, and also for his wheat crop to succeed, though knowing it likely won't. The story repeatedly uses the word 'waiting'; for instance, the woman observes that she is 'waiting for something comprehensible to jump out of this garbled mess and make sense' (p.217). Titles of short stories often convey both literal and symbolic information about the stories, and 'Waiting' is a good example of this.

There are numerous layers of symbolism in this story – which is the shortest in the collection – from the sentence level through to plot and structure. One significant example is the parallel between the protagonist waiting to have her fears confirmed (that the foetus has died) and her partner Pete waiting to see if his wheat crop will succeed. In both cases, they are certain of the worst, as the woman plans how she will manage her miscarriage *('let things take their natural course'*, p.217) and Pete plans his decision to let the cows eat the dry wheat, giving up on 'its hopeful greenness struggling in that parched ground' (p.217).

Q This story concludes before the protagonist finds out the results of the test. What do you think the result will be? Which aspects of the story lead you to think this?

Q Compare the opening and closing sentences of this story.
How do they differ, in tone and content? How does this influence your interpretation of the story's meaning?

Static (pp.219–37)

Summary: *Anthony and his wife Marie host Christmas for Anthony's family. Anthony navigates tensions between them, particularly his mother and others, and ruminates on the changes in his marriage, particularly the unspoken concern about their fertility. He urges his nephew to make a show of playing with his grandmother's gift of walkie-talkies, and they play together.*

One of the key moments in this story is when Anthony sets up the family photo. The changes in the intensity of light as he moves the camera, and particularly how this changes Marie's appearance, are extended into a metaphor that describes 'how she sees them and how they see her, this life and that life, with Anthony in the middle' (p.230). This concise moment captures many themes and central ideas of the story: Anthony's love for his family, yet his inability to resolve the enduring conflicts between their personalities; his perplexed bemusement at how Marie has changed and what their life has become; the hints, in his niece and nephew at the future of family conflicts; the extent to which he is trapped in the middle of it all, frustrated and a little lost, yet still wanting to please everyone and keep the peace.

The motif of 'rays' in this story is a good illustration of how, in much of the collection, hope and hopelessness, or positivity and despair, exist side by side. Anthony characterises the tensions and conflicts within his family (particularly between his mother and wife) as 'Evil Rays, like something in one of his old comics' (p.220): at once deadly but also childish and almost humorous, as though he is trying to diminish their power. He spends time trying to dodge these invisible, wounding tensions, and watching them injure the children, caught in the 'firing line of all those deadly rays' (p.232). Yet on the other hand, it is also the 'rays' that are 'holding them together' (p.234). This refers literally to the communication channels between the walkie-talkies but also to the fact that the tensions within families are so closely tied to the love, history and family connections they share. In a sense the positives and negatives of family life are two sides of a coin. This echoes the regular appearance together of hope and hopelessness in Kennedy's stories.

Q Choose several of Anthony's statements to Tom over the walkie-talkies. Explain their possible symbolic meaning in the context of the story.

Q This story has one of the less concrete endings in the collection. What is your understanding of the final paragraph, and how does it shape your interpretation of the story? (Consider imagery, language choices, symbolism and plot.)

Seventy-Two Derwents (pp.239–77)

Summary: *Tyler keeps a journal for school, using it to record the considerable challenges in her home life. She faces harassment and manipulation by her mother's boyfriend Shane, and even her own mother takes advantage of her, forcing her to help sew 'Plushies' to sell. Her older sister Ellie offers support and protection and eventually their mother stands up for them against the abusive Shane, demanding he leave, then defends herself and her children by stabbing him with scissors.*

This is the longest story in the collection, and differs significantly in perspective from almost all the others as it is told by a young girl on the edge of adolescence. ('Whirlpool' is the only other story with a narrator so young.) It is also different in narrative voice, as the entire story is told from Tyler's first-person perspective through the artifice of a diary. This allows for expository information and concrete statements and details that are not always present in a first-person narrative. More commonly, first-person narratives take the form of an internal monologue in which the narrator does not explicitly convey details about themselves or their situations, since the audience is effectively 'inside' the mind of the narrator. In 'Seventy-Two Derwents', on the other hand, Tyler is writing to someone who is familiar to her (her compassionate teacher, Mrs Carlyle), though outside her immediate experience, so she has an excuse to be very concrete with the information she provides her double audience – Mrs Carlyle, and the reader of the short story.

Central to 'Seventy-Two Derwents' are Tyler's conflict with her mum's boyfriend Shane and, balancing this, her supportive relationship with her older sister Ellie. A secondary narrative arc addresses the familiar theme of distance, this time between Tyler and her mother. Tyler seems financially and socially trapped, as evidenced by her simple dream of owning good-quality (Derwent) coloured pencils, and by the various behavioural pressures placed on her by her mother and Shane. However, in one significant way she is better off than any of the collection's other protagonists: she has at least one close, supportive relationship uncomplicated by conflict. Her protective bond with Ellie is an example of genuine compassion, providing a contrast to the many situations of loneliness in which the central characters of other stories find themselves, even – sometimes especially – when they are in relationships or actively involved with their families.

Mrs Carlyle and Aunty Jacinta, too (and, in the end, even Tyler's mother), are portrayed as supportive figures. This, combined with Tyler being one of the collection's youngest characters, and also the fact that this is the final story in the collection, highlights hope as one of the most enduring values underlying Kennedy's collection.

Q What is the impact of placing the longest story at the end of the collection? Think about how the other stories have shaped your expectations about events, characters and themes. How might you have interpreted this story differently if it were the first one you had read in the collection?

Q Tyler's mother is one of the characters in the collection who changes significantly. She becomes a positive force in her daughters' lives after having been initially unsupportive. How does Kennedy portray this character development?

CHARACTERS & RELATIONSHIPS

Studying and discussing characters in a collection of short stories can be a little different from working with characters in novels or plays. Often it is more useful to discuss groups of character types, and to explore how an author presents particular types of people. These might be grouped according to their most significant relationships with others, or the social role that seems to most strongly define their identity. For example, you might look at the following groups in a text:

- mothers or fathers
- friends
- husbands or wives / couples
- strangers
- children.

In some collections it might be more appropriate to group characters according to the kinds of narrative roles they play, by discussing, for instance:

- heroes or villains
- survivors
- protagonists and secondary characters.

At other times you might find it helpful to talk about pairs of character types, to discuss the contrasting ways that the author examines particular ideas through characters. For example, you might look at:

- happy or unhappy characters
- 'moral' or 'immoral' characters (though remember that this type of grouping is always subjective, so you will also need to talk about *why* you have characterised people as one or the other)
- successful or unsuccessful characters (as above, note that you would need to carefully define these sorts of categories).

There are many other possible categorisations, such as age, gender, occupation, goals and objectives, or relationship status. You might even group characters according to species, if the collection includes nonhuman characters – for example, in alternate reality or science fiction; or where animals are central to the narrative. To some extent the style and content of the collection you study will help determine the way you group characters for analysis, but it is also open to your own interpretation.

For this text guide, characters have been grouped primarily according to their roles within families. Alternatively you could look at Kennedy's characters through other frames, such as their stage in life or their vocational status. A helpful activity would be to make lists of the main characters from each story, and summarise their key details (age, close relationships, occupation, ambitions, personal qualities). You can then identify common details that will help you to choose groupings before you analyse the text. You could use tables created in your notebook or electronically, or you might try brainstorming character groups in class.

Also remember that, although it is useful to discuss character types, in your analysis you will need to provide detailed textual evidence to support any argument you offer. At times it will be important to identify specific characters from separate stories and discuss them individually, in terms of relationships, conflicts, key events, outcomes and values.

Married couples / partners

Key quotes

'Very little eye contact these days, my wife.' ('Like a House on Fire', p.74)

'My husband is an undemonstrative man and that gesture, as he fitted his warm arms and legs around me in the narrow bed, made me see how much he understood.' ('Waiting', p.216)

'Oh, it wears us thin, marriage. It knocks the edges off us.' ('Waiting', p.216)

'She flashes him a smile as she heads for the door. The ghost of an old smile, one he misses ...' ('Static', p.226)

Note that in Kennedy's stories it is not necessarily stated that couples (such as Christine and Al in 'Tender') are actually married. While there is little difference between a marriage and a partnership in these stories, remember that it is important to be precise about such details when you are analysing and writing about a text. While it may not matter, in the wider scheme of things, whether two characters are a couple or are married, if you make an assumption and use terms such as 'married', 'husband' or 'wife' when there is no evidence for this in the text, you will be revealing that you have not attended closely to the textual details, and indeed you may be making other more significant errors if this is the case.

The importance of relationships

Although many of the marriages and partnerships in the stories are not happy – whether due to conflict, unresolvable difference, or simply loss of connection over time – the collection still suggests that love and companionship are important. It does so by placing relationships at the centre of the majority of the stories, and showing that those characters who do not have partners usually wish they did (though admittedly sometimes they desire simply to prove something to their exes).

- Chris (in 'Ashes') misses his ex-partner: he 'longed so much to be with Scott that it almost hurt' ('Ashes', p.20).
- In 'Cross-Country' Rebecca's entire narrative revolves around the loss of her relationship.

- Ray in 'Sleepers' has been unable to let go of his ex, Sharon, even though his memories of her are less than positive, and he spends time thinking about trying to do something to impress her.

While it could be argued that these are examples of people simply wanting what they don't have, there are few clear instances of the opposite aspiration: couples in relationships wishing they weren't. In 'Flexion', Mrs Slovak tentatively considers that her life might be better without her husband, thinking 'it almost seems their best option' if Frank were not to survive after his accident (p.5). Certainly there is sadness in many of the other relationships, and circumstances have made characters such as Claire ('Like a House on Fire'), Roley ('Little Plastic Shipwreck') and Anthony ('Static') find their relationships particularly difficult, but even these characters do not consider separation as a better option. Michelle ('Five-Dollar Family') seems to embrace her impending independence (although it is circumstance, rather than her own actions, that prompts it), accepting the challenge of single parenthood as preferable to life with Des, who is portrayed as a no-hoper. Similarly, Tyler's mother ('Seventy-Two Derwents') finally ends her problematic relationship with Shane, recognising that it isn't working out. However, these examples are in the minority among the characters in the collection, suggesting that even imperfect romantic relationships are preferable to none.

Key point

The characters in these stories who are single are largely unhappy with this status – often because their romantic relationships recently broke down (as in 'Cross-Country' and 'Sleepers'). There are few central adult characters who are single and content: even though relationships are shown to be difficult, the experiences of the single characters suggests that relationships are still worth aspiring to.

Unhappy relationships

Unhappiness between partners in this collection is the most common experience; no central character is in an entirely happy relationship. Even among the secondary characters, only Mandy and Jake (the artists in

'White Spirit') seem to have a relationship that is free from conflict (such as the direct conflict between the couple in the title story) or externally imposed difficulty (such as the head injury sustained by Roley's wife Liz in 'Little Plastic Shipwreck', and the subsequent pressure this puts on them both). That Mandy and Jake are such minor characters supports the idea that unhappiness in relationships is the norm, with contentment a rare exception.

Yet the collection still endorses the value of relationships, demonstrating that, even within imperfect marriages and partnerships there are flashes of genuine joy, warmth, love, connectedness and shared history. These are sometimes key moments in the stories, emphasising their significance within the lives of the characters. Examples include:

- the final image in 'Flexion'
- the scene in 'Like a House on Fire' where Claire eases her husband's pain with the 'back-cracking trick' (p.91), and they find a gentle, genuine reconciliation (even if it may be 'temporary', as Claire says, referring to the pain relief but symbolically alluding to their relationship)
- although it is unfortunately ironic, Andrew's well-meaning gesture of care and kindness to Liz, buying her cake to celebrate her return to work in 'Cake'
- the memory of Pete climbing into bed with his wife in the hospital as they both share the grief of losing a baby in 'Waiting'.

Other relationships

Key quotes

'... the thought of trying to get a conversation going with any of them felt like heavy lifting.' ('Sleepers', p.134)

'They're doing their best, they're being as sisterly as they can. She must try, she really has to.' ('Cake', p.168)

While many of the stories feature characters whose key relationships are with their 'significant other', there are also examples of other kinds of close relationships, including parent–child, sibling, workplace – and even cross-species, as in the case of Roley's bond with the dolphin Samson. In most of these relationships, the patterns reflect those of the marriages and couples; conflicts, disconnections and external factors all cause rifts and tensions, yet there are moments of support and connection that are so significant as to be key incidents in the stories. Examples of these contrasting moments of connection include:

- the instant when the sisters make eye contact – in silent, united defiance of their mother – in 'Whirlpool' (p.151)
- the connection 'the scholar' makes with Mr Moreton ('Laminex and Mirrors')
- Anthony's fondness for and protectiveness of his nephew Tom ('Static').

Notably absent in this collection is any significant representation of committed friendship, with only incidental examples occurring, such as Tyler's friendship with Georgia ('Seventy-Two Derwents') and Ray living in his mate's shed ('Sleepers'). Often, instead, characters are largely disconnected from the social world around them. This suggests that Kennedy believes romantic partnerships and family to be the most significant relationships in people's lives.

Young characters

Key quotes

'You're barely twelve, you're nowhere near old enough for that.' ('Whirlpool', p.147)

'When I get to high school I want to do art in the art room where they have easels.' ('Seventy-Two Derwents', p.253)

Four of the stories feature significantly younger narrators than the others: 'Laminex and Mirrors', 'Five-Dollar Family' (although Michelle's age is not provided, she is portrayed as a young new mother), 'Whirlpool' and 'Seventy-Two Derwents'. These stories share themes and emotional tones with many of the others, and thus the collection suggests that many of its concerns – such as isolation, disadvantage and hope – are universal human experiences, regardless of age. Youth is often associated with optimism, possibility, freedom and energy, but in this collection the younger characters are no more representative of hope and freedom than any other characters. In these stories, 'the scholar', Michelle, Anna and Tyler all experience restrictions (just as the older characters do), whether financial, emotional or situational. Yet they all find reasons for hope (again, like the older characters), suggesting that human resilience is a quality that is more nature than nurture: it is present early in life.

Tyler, one of the youngest characters and the one explored in the most detail (as 'Seventy-Two Derwents' is the longest story), illustrates this idea strongly. Tyler's situation is far from ideal: she doesn't really know most of her siblings, her mother struggles to support them financially and emotionally, and her interest in art is not supported at home or at school. Moreover, she is bullied and blackmailed by her mother's boyfriend, whom the story strongly hints may have tried to abuse Tyler's elder sister, Ellie. Yet Tyler looks forward to her future and embraces the opportunities available to her, appreciating the extra concern offered by her teacher at school and holding on to her simple hopes (symbolised by her dream of owning a full set of Derwent pencils).

There are several younger figures among the secondary characters in the collection too, such as Anthony's niece and nephew Tom and Hannah in 'Static'. He notes that his mother only likes children when they're babies, because 'by the time they're Tom's and Hannah's age they've learned to be wary and submissive and not to trust her, and who can blame them' (p.233). This presents a slightly different perspective on the collection's overriding idea that both despair and hope are innate human characteristics, instead suggesting that perhaps they are learned behaviours acquired early, before adolescence.

Families

Key quotes

'... ardent rush of helpless, terrible love.' ('Tender', p.65)

'You're all touching and it feels weird.' ('Whirlpool', p.150)

The word 'family' has broad meaning and is open to numerous interpretations. For this discussion, a family group is defined as one in which at least a parent and offspring (either youthful or grown) are present. Of course, 'family' does not always involve children but in these stories, those couples who do not have children (for example the Slovaks in 'Flexion') are presented as having different relationships from those who do; the dynamics are those of a couple rather than a larger group. Such relationships are explored in 'Married couples / partners' earlier in this section.

In many of the stories, we come to know the protagonists in the context of their position within their family. In some cases these family relationships play a central role in the narrative, frequently offering the source of the driving conflict or tension. In fact there are only a few stories in which family dynamics do not figure prominently: 'Flexion', 'Laminex and Mirrors', 'Cross-Country', 'Sleepers' and 'Little Plastic Shipwreck'. Each of these instead concentrates on a key relationship between two individuals – even though this is a past, absent relationship in 'Cross-Country' and a non-romantic relationship in 'Laminex and Mirrors'. Three other stories explore ideas of family while not featuring the nuclear family structures present elsewhere. In 'White Spirit' it could be argued that the protagonist's role in the estate community resembles that of a parent, while in 'Waiting' the central couple do not yet have children, but their attempts to become parents are the focus of the story. This is also a secondary focus in 'Static'. The frequency with which family dynamics appear throughout the text helps to convey the idea that family relationships underlie and inform all life experiences.

Kennedy explores family situations from the perspectives of mothers (as in 'Tender', 'Five-Dollar Family', 'Cake' and, through secondary characters, 'Ashes' and 'Seventy-Two Derwents'), fathers ('Like a House on Fire' and, through an almost-silent secondary character, 'Whirlpool'), children ('Ashes', 'Whirlpool' and 'Seventy-Two Derwents'), and extended family relationships, such as those in 'Static'. At their simplest level, these relationships all indicate that family is important in constructing an individual's sense of self and shaping their interactions with the world.

For example, in 'Ashes', Chris' memories of his childhood are closely tied to his adult relationship with his mother, which is also influenced by the ways in which she and his father had interacted. Similarly, in 'Whirlpool' the dynamic between Anna's parents influences – and is influenced by – her own relationship with them, shown when she and her father quietly unite against her mother over the issue of the pool. In 'Static', Anthony builds an alliance with his young nephew Tom, partly to protect his mother (Tom's grandmother) and her feelings, but also to shore up strength against her interfering and frustrating ways. The complexity of this relationship illustrates how family dynamics work throughout the text: while family is a necessary and sometimes sympathetic force in these stories, it is frequently antagonistic, creating conflict and challenges for individuals.

Character types – such as mothers – are presented quite differently across the collection, showing that while familial roles shape identity, they do not define it. Kennedy also offers even-handed evaluations of various character types' positive or negative influence on others. For example, in 'Tender', Christine's own health takes a back seat to her desire to care for her children. She loses sleep building the model for Jamie, and considers the family's future without her if her diagnosis is serious, not dwelling on the possibility of her own suffering. On the other hand, in 'Static' Anthony's mother fails to really understand others (such as when she buys walkie-talkies for Tom) or to put her own needs, expectations and priorities aside; instead she brings tension, judgement and conflict to the family Christmas.

While the collection does present some very supportive family relationships (for example between Ellie and Tyler in 'Seventy-Two

Derwents'), more frequently these relationships are shown to be fraught with conflict and imperfection, suggesting that maintaining equilibrium within families is rarely easy. Examples include:

- the tensions between Chris and his mother, and the equally problematic relationship he recalls with his father ('Ashes')
- the strain between the parents in 'Like a House on Fire' when the narrator's injury prevents him from successfully fulfilling his roles within the family
- the dissolving relationship between baby Jason's parents in 'Five-Dollar Family'
- the uncomfortable family Christmas in 'Static', where habits of interpersonal conflict dominate the gathering
- Ellie and Tyler's mother's inconsistent parenting ('Seventy-Two Derwents').

There are also more complex representations of family, as in 'Cake', in which the protagonist's family members are largely absent from the events of the story, but very present in her inner thoughts. This shows, again, how important family roles and relationships are to individuals' behaviour, motivations and experiences.

Characters at turning points

Key quotes

'It doesn't matter anyway. She's got everything this baby needs, now.' ('Five-Dollar Family', p.113)

'... whatever you've been watching, ready or not, it's time to roll the credits.' ('Cross-Country', p.126)

Many of the stories take place at key moments in characters' lives. This is a common practice in short fiction, as it creates both tension and high stakes for the characters, giving readers insight into significant events and demonstrating how the characters respond to crises and how these events might change their lives. In Kennedy's collection, we rarely see the outcomes of these crises, and sometimes not even the key event itself but rather the lead-up. Often the stories end just at the moment when there is likely to be a turning point; for instance, in 'Tender', when Christine is about to find out whether her life will change dramatically (with a cancer diagnosis); in 'Waiting', when the protagonist is about to learn whether or not her pregnancy is viable; and in 'Sleepers' when Ray is about to be caught by the police.

Key point

Structurally, leaving characters' fates undetermined at the end of the story not only engages readers (by positioning them to consider the possible and likely outcomes), but also emphasises themes and ideas of the text, such as the notion of hope.

Some stories do show the completion of key moments of crisis for characters. For example:

- In 'Ashes' the key conflict is Chris' trip with his mother, and the climax is the dispersal of his father's ashes. We are left with his final symbolic action: gently brushing the smear of ash from his mother's jacket.
- In 'Laminex and Mirrors' the central tension is whether 'the scholar' will risk her job to provide some joy for Mr Moreton; the resolution occurs when she does so, and we understand that this could affect her future, as the loss of income might prevent or at least forestall her dreams of travel.
- Although in 'Five-Dollar Family' the crisis point for Des (the court case) is yet to happen, the key moment for Michelle is getting to the photography session. She achieves this, then is immediately able to breastfeed her newborn with the milk she has desperately awaited.
- In 'Seventy-Two Derwents' one of the supporting characters, Tyler's mother, responds to a very dramatic crisis point when Shane threatens the family and she strongly stands up for them and retaliates.

In these stories the essence of characters is communicated through their actions in times of extreme challenge. Such actions can be interpreted, sometimes symbolically, to reveal the underlying ideas and values of the text. Chris' final action shows that, despite his lifelong conflict with his parents and their inability to accept him for who he is, he will always remain compassionate ('Ashes'). In 'Laminex and Mirrors' we see that kindness is more important than personal desires or gains. For Michelle there is the concrete evidence of her independence: that she will be able to support herself and, more importantly, her baby, even though his father won't be there ('Five-Dollar Family'). In 'Seventy-Two Derwents' the mother has finally begun to value herself (facilitated by the success of the Plushies), and in turn learns to value and defend her family; significantly, it is with the very tools of her new self-confidence (the 'special' scissors for making the Plushies) that she finally eradicates danger (Shane) from her daughters' lives.

In other stories, the central events or tensions are mundane and minute, reminding us that much of life is the undramatic daily existence *between* key events and crises. These stories show characters having everyday experiences and, rather than highlighting their essential nature through revealing how they respond to crises, these ordinary circumstances portray individuals' stable, enduring personalities.

- In 'Like a House on Fire', although the protagonist's back injury is a crisis, this is a long-term source of conflict in his family's life, rather than a heightened moment or key event.
- In 'White Spirit', the central challenge of finalising the mural on time highlights the daily trials and frustrations of the protagonist's life and work on the estate.
- In 'Static', Anthony and his family manifest long-term discontentment with each other. Although Christmas brings their feelings to a head, there is no sense that this event is different from any other in their shared lives; rather, this is a sketch of the tensions continuously challenging them.

These instances give the reader a sense of glimpsing the characters in unguarded moments, and observing the patterns and relationships that most accurately illustrate the characters' lives.

THEMES, IDEAS & VALUES

Disadvantage

Key quotes

'Her children, perfect, made with her own once-trustworthy body.' ('Tender', p.70)

'It's triple pay if I work overnight on Christmas Eve.' ('Like a House on Fire', p.79)

'… laughing feels like panting for breath, remembering what it's like to be fit.' ('Like a House on Fire', p.89)

'Her money, her baby allowance, already gone … when she hasn't even got a change table.' ('Five-Dollar Family', p.109)

The characters in the stories frequently face disadvantages that require energy to overcome, or that restrict their emotional and practical freedoms. Disadvantage comes in many forms throughout the collection, but two of the most commonly represented are financial and physical.

Financial challenges

In several stories, financial struggles contribute to the tensions between characters or to their underlying motivations or aspirations. Financial distress is rarely the sole cause of unhappiness (though in 'Cake' it is the primary reason Liz returns to work and, in turn, her separation from her young son is the primary reason for her distress), but is often shown to be a factor. Tyler's family ('Seventy-Two Derwents') and Michelle ('Five-Dollar Family') provide the clearest illustrations of the stress that financial disadvantage can place upon individuals and families.

On the other hand, the collection also indicates that many characters and families who are reasonably well-off are still desperately unhappy. This supports the adage that 'money can't buy happiness'; the text, as a whole, endorses the notion that social, emotional and interpersonal wellbeing are at least as important as financial wealth. A strong illustration of this idea can be seen in 'Static', when Anthony's wealth is juxtaposed with his sister Margaret's family's struggles. They are in 'dire financial straits' while he and Marie have a 'big new house' and can afford to buy expensive Christmas presents for their niece and nephew (p.227). However, Anthony and Marie's relationship is strained and rocky, while in the family photo at Christmas he describes 'Margaret, kind and comfortable, touching Ian's arm and smiling warmly' even while she is 'overweight and worn and dowdy … frumpy beside the immaculate blonde Marie' (p.230). Kennedy demonstrates that while money may add polish and shine to the exterior of a relationship, it is no match for genuine connection, which can survive even financial trauma.

Physical challenges

A number of stories focus on the difficulties faced by individuals (and their partners and families) who experience forms of physical trauma. These characters include:

- Frank ('Flexion')
- Mr Moreton and the other patients ('Laminex and Mirrors')
- Christine ('Tender')
- the protagonist in 'Like a House on Fire'
- Liz ('Little Plastic Shipwreck')
- the protagonist in 'Waiting'.

In several stories the bodily challenges are less central but still relevant, such as Marie and Anthony's fertility struggle ('Static'), or the sexual abuse hinted at in 'Seventy-Two Derwents'. Other characters, too, are influenced by the demands and challenges of their physical selves. For example, Michelle ('Five-Dollar Family') overcomes the physical uncertainty of becoming a new mother; for Anna ('Whirlpool'), her weight is a delicate issue as she enters adolescence unsupported by her family; and Liz ('Cake'), who is weaning her son, 'craves' the bodily weight of him 'on the crook of her hip … she's unbalanced without it … weirdly light and empty' (p.166).

The physical distress or disadvantage in most stories is usually responsible for creating tensions, conflict and difficulty within interpersonal relationships (particularly marriages), thus endorsing the notion that physical wellbeing is necessary for emotional wellbeing.

At the same time, however, sometimes the physical trauma can bring about the greatest moments of compassion and tenderness between people – as in the final moments of 'Flexion'. This reflects the broader idea in the collection that from challenge can come strength. A vivid example is the climax of 'Seventy-Two Derwents', during which Tyler and Ellie's mum stands up to the direct corporeal threat posed by Shane, finally breaking the cycle of tension and conflict in the household.

Isolation and loneliness

Key quotes

'That's Frank all over. Can't hold a fork, but can still find a way to smack her out of the way.' ('Flexion', p.7)

'... the lifetime habit of keeping his responses to himself closed his mouth in a firm and well-worn line. A line that suggested nothing, broached nothing, gave nothing away.' ('Ashes', p.19)

'... I feel the heavy dish of water in my chest teeter and almost overbalance, and I ache with holding it steady.' ('Waiting', p.218)

While very few characters in the collection are entirely alone (in the sense of not having active connections with family, partners, friends or work colleagues), many are lonely. Similarly, while characters are rarely physically isolated (in the sense of living in remote geographical locations, or being removed from social contact with others), they often lack support networks or hold their pain to themselves rather than sharing it with those close to them. Emotional isolation is a theme that runs through most of the stories, often underlying the key conflicts and events. Indeed, it is introduced in the very first story, indicating, structurally, that the idea of isolation will be a central concern.

In 'Flexion' Mrs Slovak's emotional isolation is long-term and has shaped her quiet longing for a life other than her own. It is linked with the extent of control her husband Frank has over her life – Frank, 'who'd rather cut off his own hand than be beholden to anyone' (p.4). When she and Frank lost their baby, he decreed that they would put the event behind them and that 'nobody was to know' (p.5), enforcing for them both a social and emotional isolation that matches their rural isolation (this is one of the few stories in which the environmental setting reflects the theme of isolation).

The key crisis in this story is Frank's serious injury and the subsequent challenges of recovery. Frank's past independence, however, does not come back to punish them, as we might expect. Rather, the severity of his trauma draws neighbours and tradespeople to offer support in the form of practical services, including gifts of food and modifications to the house. This could be interpreted in several ways. On the one hand, it could be seen as evidence for the belief that individuals have greater social resources than they are aware of, until they have extreme needs – isolation is often self-imposed, and trauma can force a breakthrough. On the other hand, it could be read as emphasising the fact that, despite the practical support offered, Mrs Slovak is still very lonely, reminding us that loneliness is not only the domain of single people, and can be equally devastating for individuals within relationships. Both interpretations support the view that companionship is important, as independence necessarily brings with it the often-damaging experience of isolation.

Emotional isolation is similarly connected to other stories' central events and central messages. In 'Cross-Country', Rebecca decides, after her break-up, to 'wrap' herself 'in the spare-room quilt' and isolate herself from the offers of support from friends (p.116). She also avoids work obligations, instead immersing herself in the unhealthy (and ultimately unproductive) solo pursuit of online stalking, to try to find out what her ex is now doing. Without external support, her anger and hurt resulting from the break-up cannot be healed.

In several stories, women experience physical suffering or at least fear, and lack the inclination, capacity or opportunity to share their worries with their partners or families. For example, in 'Tender', 'Five-Dollar Family' and 'Waiting', the protagonists are anticipating negative news regarding health concerns or (in Michelle's case) life events, and even when they are shown to have supportive relationships (as in 'Tender' and 'Waiting'), they choose not to share their worries with their partners and instead manage the experiences alone.

These stories are told from the first-person ('Waiting') and third-person limited ('Tender', 'Five-Dollar Family') perspectives, both narrative points of view that tend to draw readers closely into the protagonists' experiences and state of mind. In this way, Kennedy emphasises the loneliness that can come with personal suffering when it is not shared. 'Like a House on Fire' is also told in the first person, putting the reader in the position of the protagonist and encouraging us to empathise with his physical suffering which, despite his wife's support, has become very private due to its protracted nature. In fact, most of the stories focus on characters' internal perspectives (none is told from the third-person omniscient viewpoint, for example), which brings an intimate focus to the protagonists' narratives, increasing the sense that many of them are struggling through their personal trials in a very isolated, individual way.

The disappointment of reality

Key quotes

'... his mother has embellished past events to give them a patina of something richer and happier.' ('Ashes', p.26)

'It's amazing, isn't it, the level to which we'll invent what we need.' ('Cross-Country', p.125)

Recurrent in these stories is the contrast between how characters want, hope or expect their worlds to be, and how they actually are. Most often, the reality is a disappointment rather than an improvement. The characters in the following list are each faced with glum realities following either brief or extended periods of bright optimism. Their experiences can be read as a warning against raising one's hopes too far, as they will invariably fail to be fulfilled, leading to regret and sorrow.

- Mrs Slovak ('Flexion') imagines a new, freer life if Frank dies from his injuries, but instead he survives, tying her to an even more difficult existence than she had before.
- 'The scholar' in 'Laminex and Mirrors' expects to save up 'enough for three months in Europe' (p.39) but, after her escapade with Mr Moreton, this will no longer be a reality.
- In 'Tender', Christine reflects on the idyllic life she and Al thought they would build – she had 'fantasies' of living a life with 'a golden halo of lamplight ... everything as clean and wholesome as a cake of handmade soap' (p.58) – while her reality is harshly different, and far less satisfying.
- In 'Sleepers', Ray imagines using some of the sleepers to landscape the garden for himself and Sharon, but instead is arrested while stealing them.
- The mother in 'Whirlpool' expects a perfect professional family photo but, unbeknown to her, her daughters have sabotaged it – this minor event is an analogy for the idea of reality or actual outcomes being a let-down.
- In 'White Spirit', the minister expects (and indeed perceives) a grand, 'authentic' community success with the mural (p.192), but, in an example of dramatic irony, the readers know that the community has not really taken ownership of the mural – in fact, the protagonist has had to have it coated with a sealant (symbolically 'glossing over' the truth) to prevent it being vandalised.

However, in a number of instances there are moments of great positivity arising from reality. For example, despite the fact that 'the scholar' knows her aspirations have been compromised, she identifies the moment following the story's climax (locked outside after taking Mr Moreton out for a cigarette) as 'the one I remember most clearly from the year I turned eighteen' and describes it as a 'perfect moment', full of laughter and freedom (p.56). She could not have foreseen this event, and it is an improvement on her plans and expectations for that summer. Despite the disappointing reality, the unexpected and unplanned-for moment is sometimes the best one.

Despair

Key quotes

'I go to the spot I always do, like a beaten dog.' ('Like a House on Fire', p.77)

'People who tell you to get out and move on, they're standing there in a thick layer of skin, cushioned and comfortable, brimming with their easy clichés like something off a desk calendar.' ('Cross-Country', p.115)

'... these endless, extended moments where you're left in limbo, the time dangling like a suspended toy on a piece of elastic.' ('Cake', p.165)

In most of these stories, we see characters facing despair. While most do not fully sink into desperation, it is ever-present. In keeping with the collection's domestic tone and settings, the characters experience desolation on a small, intimate, personal scale. Their unhappiness is often caused by physical pain or injury. The characters' fears and worries usually concern life – that is, the daily trials of modern existence in a developed world – rather than mortality.

Despair is often the result of acknowledging the passing of time and the changing of relationships, such as in 'Static' when Anthony recalls his wife when she was carefree and 'unselfconscious. Years ago' (p.226). At other times it may be a response to a difficult situation, such as the Slovaks' experience after Frank's accident ('Flexion'), or what Michelle faces as a new – and imminently single – mother after her son is born ('Five-Dollar Family'). Often it is the existential frustration and dread of facing a mundane future as demonstrated by Ray's stagnant life in 'Sleepers' and, in 'Cake', the protagonist's depression at returning to work when she would rather be with her son. It is also present in many other stories as characters cope with the monotonous realities of daily life.

Key point

Not just humans but animals and inanimate objects are described in terms of despair. In 'Little Plastic Shipwreck', 'poor Rex' the sea-lion is blinded with cataracts and despondent in his enclosure, 'like a big fat kid alone on the slide' while the turtles have the 'hateful, icy glare of an old drunk' (p.202). In 'Static' even furniture is personified: 'the lounge chair exhales a gust of weary depression' (p.224).

Hope and tenacity

Key quotes

'She places his hand wordlessly, determinedly, over his heart, and holds it there.' ('Flexion', p.16)

'One day I will get an aviary and then I will come and get her ... That's my promise.' ('Seventy-Two Derwents', p.277)

Despite the collection's overwhelming tones of despair, there are also indelible signs of hope in most of the stories, indicating that the human determination to carry on, and to find the potential for good in even the most difficult circumstances, is strong. Sometimes this optimism is revealed in minute gestures or events, such as the Slovaks' cautious affection at the end of 'Flexion', Chris' gentle touch of care for his mother at the end of 'Ashes', and the rare instance of unity between Anna and Louise in 'Whirlpool'. These moments tend to occur in the conclusions of the stories, leaving the reader with an optimistic image. Thus even when the moments of hope are tiny, they carry narrative weight – due to their structural position – that can often balance the predominantly bleak tone of the individual stories. At other times the idea of hope is presented symbolically in small details embedded in stories, as in 'Like a House on Fire' when the baby Jesus is the only part of the nativity not broken.

Key point

Remember that details like this are neither coincidence nor accidental but always carefully constructed by the author. In the example of the nativity scene, for instance, if instead the donkey or the manger remained unbroken, the symbolism would have been quite different. But it is the baby – not just any baby, but baby Jesus, a strong religious and cultural symbol – who survives the accident. This symbolises how underneath the apparent wreckage of the protagonist's personal and family life, there lies the possibility of a better future: something innocent, undamaged and full of potential, just like a baby.

The possibility of change

One of the ways in which the collection illustrates the theme of hope is to show that, despite the difficulties characters face, there is potential for development and improvement. For example, in 'Five-Dollar Family' Michelle is overwhelmed by the emotional and bodily pressures of supporting her new baby, and of knowing that she will be doing so without his father. At the beginning of the story, she is having trouble waking and feeding Jason, but the climax of the narrative occurs when her milk comes in, showing us that she will be able to physically support Jason. This suggests that she will, after all, be able to manage motherhood even though for much of the story it seems almost impossible for her. Another example is in 'Cross-Country': most of the story shows us the protagonist trapped in her misery, removed from her daily life and struggling to cope with the loss of her relationship. But as the story concludes she shuts down her computer, preparing to have a shower. These actions suggest that she is at a turning point and will be moving on from her period of despair.

Perhaps the strongest illustration of the possibility of change is the climax of 'Seventy-Two Derwents', when the girls' mother takes dramatic action to protect her family and make way for change. As this is the concluding story in the collection, it asserts firmly that change is possible and that no situation, no matter how difficult, is permanent.

Resilience

Kennedy shows us characters who don't give up, no matter what life throws in their way. Thus, the collection endorses the values of persistence, perseverance and hope. Each of the protagonists is portrayed during a time of personal challenge, whether temporary – as in 'White Spirit' – or longer-term – as in 'Flexion'. Yet not one of them gives in. The fact that each story presents this pattern conveys an underlying affirmation of human resilience and strength.

Ordinariness

Key quotes

'… the space bar, measuring out a million incremental small spaces.' ('Cake', p.159)

'But I'm not a martyr, just someone who can see what needs doing, and does it.' ('Waiting', p.216)

Rarely do these stories have high dramatic stakes – though the personal emotional stakes are often high. Their climaxes tend to involve conflict between or even within individuals. The risks taken are often minimal, in the scheme of the worlds the characters inhabit. The events and settings are primarily domestic. In terms of careers, interests, behaviour and qualities, the people in the stories are believable and unremarkable. There are no dramatic heroes and villains; rather, the characters are the sorts of people many of us encounter in our daily lives. They are men and women who go about their routine existences, encountering challenges and tensions that affect them personally, for days or years, but who are unlikely to change the wider world very much.

This differs from many other texts you might read, in which the focus might be on dramatic events or extraordinary characters. In *Like a House on Fire*, what is important is the minutia of contemporary life: the moment-to-moment thoughts and feelings of ordinary people. This is observable at various levels of the text's construction: in the settings and events as well as in the style of writing. The timescales are generally small, and symbolic and linguistic details are important. The focus is on the intricate rather than the 'big picture'.

In her emphasis on the ordinary, Kennedy suggests that these small, relatively unimportant (on a global scale) details are the heart of human experience. The ideas that dominate the narratives in this collection are the challenges of interacting with other humans, and of managing one's own relationship with the world. The message offered again and again in the stories is that life is never smooth yet humans find ways to cope.

DIFFERENT INTERPRETATIONS

Different interpretations arise from different responses to a text. Over time, a text will evoke a wide range of responses from its readers, who may come from various social or cultural groups and live in very different places and historical periods. Responses by critics and reviewers can be published in newspapers, journals and books, both online and in print. They can also be expressed in discussions among readers in the media, classrooms, book groups and so on.

While there is no single correct reading or interpretation of a text, it is important to understand that an interpretation is more than a personal opinion – it is the justification of a point of view on the text. To present an interpretation of a text based on your point of view, you must use a logical argument and support it with relevant evidence from the text.

The critics' viewpoints

Reading critical responses to your text can help your study of the text by identifying ideas, themes and textual features that you might want to analyse more deeply in your own discussions of the work. You might find responses that identify themes you had not considered, and you might even find responses with which you disagree. Don't worry about this, as it is an excellent way to stimulate your own thinking and analysis. If you disagree with a review, try to come up with a supported argument against it, providing examples from the text to substantiate your point of view.

Critical responses include reviews published in respected online or print sources such as newspapers and literary journals. Informal but considered personal responses, such as those published in literary blogs or online literary communities or social networking sites, can also be seen as critical responses, as long as they are written in a balanced way and the writers support their opinions with textual evidence. This is another reason to seek out critical responses to your text: they will help you learn, by example, to support your own responses to the text. Try to find a range of responses to your text, including (if possible) at least some of the following:

- professional responses (i.e. those published in commercial or academic sources)
- personal responses (such as those on literary networking sites, or on regular literary blogs)
- reviews from Australia as well as other countries
- reviews from different perspectives (such as literary or social/cultural).

Also try to find positive reviews (those evaluating the text as being largely successful) as well as negative reviews (those finding the text unsatisfactory in significant ways). Don't forget that all views must be supported by evidence. Responses that 'like' or 'dislike' a text, without presenting a strong argument as to *why*, are likely to be irrelevant and not useful. This goes for your own analysis too: the point of studying and discussing texts is not to write about whether you enjoyed it or not, but to form responses to the work and to understand how to provide textual evidence to support these responses. Note that many critical responses are likely to contain both positive and negative feedback about a text.

Below are several examples of reviews of *Like a House on Fire*, demonstrating the range suggested above, and citing an example of the way the response uses textual evidence to support its perspective. (Note that because this text is contemporary, you will not be able to find a range of historical responses. Similarly, as it is a work from a relatively small Australian publisher, you are unlikely to find many international reviews.)

James Ley in *The Australian* – a professional, commercial review, with an evaluation leaning towards the *negative*

Regular literary critic Ley's review commends the craft and quality of individual stories but argues overall that the collection is problematic, principally in that it lacks variation of tone, setting and style, and that instead the stories are too alike, and 'the cumulative effect is not an amplification or enrichment of her thematic preoccupations but a collective diminution' (Ley 2012). He also cynically uses an extended metaphor to illustrate how some of Kennedy's stories fail to rise above the 'formulaic' nature of the modern short story: 'take an ordinary person, add a half-cup of complicating factors and a tablespoon of emotional confusion, stir gently until they arrive at a moment of realisation, pour the contents into a symbolic bowl and sprinkle with tasteful imagery'.

The judges' reports from the Stella Prize and the Steele Rudd Award – professional, non-commercial reviews, with *positive* evaluations

Both these reports (released by panels, not individual judges) summarise the reason for the collection's inclusion in their respective shortlists/ prizes; obviously, due to the context of the responses, their emphasis is on the successful elements of the work. Note, however, that both reports (while very short) focus on different elements of the collection. For example, the Stella report (2013) suggests the importance of reading the collection as a whole, not just as individual stories, praising the collection for being 'more that just the sum of its parts; it's as though the various characters from the different stories could pass each other in the street every day'. The Steele Rudd report (2013), on the other hand, prioritises an assessment of the techniques and language choices: 'however dark the territory, Kennedy's take on life is marked by humour. Her style is strong and expansive and lifts beyond its realist roots to reveal a master's love of language'.

Jennifer Mills in *Overland* – a professional review, from a cultural perspective, with a mostly *positive* evaluation

Overland is an Australian cultural and literary journal. Mills, an Australian writer, examines the collection as a work of 'domestic fiction', arguing that the term is problematic (since it has almost derogatory connotations for female writers) but that Kennedy extends the conventions of this style, justifying a re-evaluation of the term. Mills asserts that 'Kennedy manages to make our domestic and corporeal realities seem as urgent and essential as they are in our lived experience' (Mills 2013). Mills identifies details of particular stories to support her argument about the collection's focus on physical bodies and experience: 'often the resolution of these stories is through gesture, movement, a physical touch. A man brushes something from his mother's sleeve; arms reach around a woman's body; a drop of blood rises to the surface of a finger'. The review concludes by proclaiming that Kennedy 'is not reduced by the domestic; rather, she makes the domestic stretch to contain all we know of mercy and redemption and humanity. There's no more universal authority than this'.

Jessica White in her own blog – a personal/peer review, with a mainly *positive* evaluation

White is a peer of Kennedy's – a fellow contemporary, award-winning Australian novelist. White (2013) concentrates on the literary quality of the collection. She notes themes (such as poverty) in *Like a House on Fire* that recur in other of Kennedy's works, and examines examples of key events and relationships in the collection, as well as discussing language features (such as point of view and metaphor). Having presented detailed textual evidence as examples, White concludes that the collection is versatile and engaging.

Two interpretations

The following interpretations demonstrate how the similar observations can be used to sustain two contrasting interpretations of the text, as long as this judgement is supported with evidence from that text.

Interpretation 1: *Like a House on Fire* suggests that humanity is a catalogue of daily burdens.

In this collection, story after story shows the pain, suffering and stress that humans experience in their day-to-day lives. Some stories look at emotional traumas such as the loss of a loved one ('Ashes') or the break-up of a relationship ('Cross-Country' or 'Sleepers'). In these instances, the loss or break-up dominates the entire story, demonstrating the pervasive misery such events bring. In others the distress is physical – for instance, when characters must learn to live with disability or chronic pain ('Flexion' or the title story), or are facing illness ('Tender') or struggling with issues relating to reproduction (Michelle has difficulty at first, feeding her newborn in 'Five-Dollar Family'; while others struggle to have children, as in 'Waiting' and 'Static'). Often, too, the things that bring frustration and worry are the simple existential facts of contemporary life, such as the tedium of work in 'Cake'. The fact that central characters vary in age, gender and circumstances shows that the mundane challenges of humanity are widespread.

Language choices as well as plot events in the collection support a reading of the text as an illustration of human burden. Throughout, there is frequent imagery of the plodding, heavy, painful nature of daily life, whether in simple repetition of tasks or by moments that are more distressing than usual. The text provides numerous examples that you could quote to support such a reading.

For example, in the title story, implying that the protagonist's identity has shrunk to fit into his injured spinal disc, the couple's brief practical interchanges are 'the extent of how we communicate these days, in the tiny squeezed and inflamed gap somewhere between slippage and rupture' (p.79). In 'Five-Dollar Family', Michelle thinks of herself, and her life, as 'numb on the outside, and a burning ache inside' (p.110). The protagonist of 'Waiting' has a 'heart like a shallow dish of water I was desperate not to tip' (p.214).

'Cake' contains numerous quotations on the subject, including 'a whole afternoon to go ... stretching before her like an endurance run' (p.171) and 'she can't believe how the meeting drags, plodding ponderously through item after laborious item ... the day yawning ahead with tiny variations' (p.173). In 'Seventy-Two Derwents', Tyler describes fear in various ways, including: 'sometimes I feel like I have a stone inside my stomach' (p.255).

No stories in the collection portray characters at happy times in their lives, other than those illustrating the ordeals that can accompany traditionally joyful events such as Christmas or the birth of children. This does not suggest that humans never experience happy times. Rather, the collection's emphasis on the difficult moments in life is evidence that such trials are a quintessential element of human existence.

Interpretation 2: The stories in *Like a House on Fire* show that even in the midst of despair there is room for optimism.

Each of Kennedy's stories in this collection features a particularly distressing period for its central character – whether that distress is as severe as the death of a parent ('Ashes') or creature ('Little Plastic Shipwreck') or the fear of a potentially serious medical result ('Tender' or 'Waiting'); or less life-threatening, such as the heightened tensions accompanying a family photography session ('Five-Dollar Family' or 'Whirlpool'), or a first day back at work for a new mother ('Cake'). What is important about these difficult key incidents and periods, however, is how each character not only survives them, but often shows evidence of beginning to thrive, as Tyler's family look set to do, after her mother stands up for them at last (albeit violently). In emerging from trauma or moving on from unhappiness, the characters provide evidence of hope and show that, even in the midst of despair, there is room for optimism.

The collection provides this evidence in three main ways: through plot elements, through narrative structure and through the use of imagery and symbolism. Examples of the kinds of textual evidence you might use to support this reading include the following.

Plot elements

- Michelle's breast milk comes in as her baby's father is set to leave ('Five-Dollar Family').
- The protagonist unexpectedly both finds and provides joy in her hospital job ('Laminex and Mirrors').

Structural evidence

- The collection as a whole begins with a tragedy (the accident beginning 'Flexion') but ends with a sense of new beginnings: Tyler is about to start a new school, her final words are about the idea of a baby bird, and she makes a promise for the future – all these elements ensure that the collection moves from tragedy to (admittedly cautious) optimism.
- Individual stories frequently end with positive imagery or language, leaving the reader with hope instead of distress, even when the key events and mood have been bleak – for example, 'Cross-Country' concludes with Rebecca closing Windows (this is also symbolic), putting that troubled time of her life into the past.

Symbolism

- In the title story although the protagonist accidentally smashes the nativity scene, the baby Jesus – a religious icon of hope – remains undamaged.
- When Tyler's mother attacks Shane, she uses the new scissors, a symbol of the family's emerging independence and self-respect (since she has used them to make the Plushies and earn money).

QUESTIONS & ANSWERS

This section focuses on your own analytical writing on the text, and gives you strategies for producing high quality responses in your coursework and exam essays.

Essay writing – an overview

An essay is a formal and serious piece of writing that presents your point of view on the text, usually in response to a given essay topic. Your 'point of view' in an essay is your interpretation of the meaning of the text's language, structure, characters, situations and events, supported by detailed analysis of textual evidence.

Analyse – don't summarise

In your essays it is important to avoid simply summarising what happens in a text.

- A **summary** is a description or paraphrase (retelling in different words) of the characters and events. For example: 'Macbeth has a horrifying vision of a dagger dripping with blood before he goes to murder King Duncan'.
- An **analysis** is an explanation of the real meaning or significance that lies 'beneath' the text's words (and images, for a film). For example: 'Macbeth's vision of a bloody dagger shows how deeply uneasy he is about the violent act he is contemplating – as well as his sense that supernatural forces are impelling him to act'.

A limited amount of summary is sometimes necessary to let your reader know which part of the text you wish to discuss. However, always keep this to a minimum and follow it immediately with your analysis (explanation) of what this part of the text is really telling us.

Plan your essay

Carefully plan your essay so that you have a clear idea of what you are going to say. The plan ensures that your ideas flow logically, that your argument remains consistent and that you stay on the topic. An essay plan should be a list of **brief dot points** – no more than half a page.

- Include your central argument or main contention – a concise statement (usually in a single sentence) of your overall response to the topic. See 'Analysing a Sample Topic' for guidelines on how to formulate a main contention.
- Write three or four dot points for each paragraph, indicating the main idea and evidence/examples from the text. Note that in your essay you will need to *expand* on these points and *analyse* the evidence.

Structure your essay

An essay is a complete, self-contained piece of writing. It has a clear beginning (the introduction), middle (several body paragraphs) and end (the last paragraph or conclusion). It must also have a central argument that runs throughout, linking each paragraph to form a coherent whole.

See examples of introductions and conclusions in the 'Analysing a Sample Topic' and 'Sample Answer' sections.

The introduction establishes your overall response to the topic. It includes your main contention and outlines the main evidence you will refer to in the course of the essay. Write your introduction *after* you have done a plan and *before* you write the rest of the essay.

The body paragraphs argue your case – they present evidence from the text and explain how this evidence supports your argument. Each body paragraph needs:

- a strong **topic sentence** (usually the first sentence) that states the main point being made in the paragraph
- **evidence** from the text, including some brief quotations
- **analysis** of the textual evidence explaining its significance and **explanation** of how it supports your argument
- **links back to the topic** in one or more statements, usually towards the end of the paragraph.

Connect the body paragraphs so that your discussion flows smoothly. Use some linking words and phrases such as 'similarly' and 'on the other hand', though don't start every paragraph like this. Another strategy is to use a significant word from the last sentence of one paragraph in the first sentence of the next.

Use key terms from the topic – or synonyms for them – throughout, so the relevance of your discussion to the topic is always clear.

The conclusion ties everything together and finishes the essay. It includes strong statements that emphasise your central argument and provide a clear response to the topic. Avoid simply restating the points made earlier in the essay – this will end on a very flat note and imply that you have run out of ideas and vocabulary. The conclusion is meant to be a logical extension of what you have written, not just a repetition or summary of it. Writing an effective conclusion can be a challenge. Try using these tips:

- Start by linking back to the final sentence of the second-last paragraph – this helps your writing to 'flow', rather than just leaping back to your main contention straight away.
- Use synonyms and expressions with equivalent meanings to vary your vocabulary. This allows you to reinforce your line of argument without being repetitive.
- When planning your essay, think of one or two broad statements or observations about the text's wider meaning. These should be related to the topic and your overall argument. Keep them for the conclusion, since they will give you something 'new' to say but still follow logically from your discussion. The introduction will be focused on the topic, but the conclusion can present a wider view of the text.

Essay topics

1. Cate Kennedy has said 'I think heroes are people who cope.'
   How do the stories in *Like a House on Fire* illustrate this statement?
2. '*Like a House on Fire* shows that family relationships are never perfect.'
   Do you agree?
3. 'The characters in these stories are all finding ways of "keeping up appearances".' Discuss.
4. The protagonist in 'White Spirit' describes herself as "a dowdy, sad sparrow among peacocks."
   How does Kennedy use figurative language to communicate her themes?
5. 'Gender plays no role in the emotional fates of the characters in *Like a House on Fire*.'
   To what extent do you agree?
6. 'The narrative points of view reveal the characters' deeply personal responses to life's challenges.' Discuss.
7. 'Characters in these stories have little control over their own lives.'
   Do you agree?
8. 'It is often the secondary characters who help convey themes in these stories.' Discuss.
9. 'In these stories, hope and despair are perfectly balanced.'
   Do you agree?
10. "The room is stiff with a charged awkwardness, with languages I can't speak."
    How does Kennedy show communication issues to be central in these stories?

Analysing a sample topic

'*Like a House on Fire* shows that family relationships are never perfect.' Do you agree?

First look at any instruction words in the topic: here you are being directly asked to agree, disagree, or partially agree with a statement about the text. Next identify and define key terms relating to the text: here you would underline 'shows' (which tells you to look at elements of the text's construction to explain how it can 'show' anything to readers), 'family relationships' (indicating which characters and relationships you will need to focus on) and 'never perfect' (this points you to the thematic areas you will be exploring).

Pay close attention to words like 'never' or 'always' that appear in a topic, as these will shape your response and often encourage you to explore a 'partially agree' answer, since an 'agree' answer in this case will mean that you would need to argue that there is not a single illustration of a perfect family relationship within the text. A 'partially agree' response can be easy in that it allows you to look at both sides of an argument, but remember that you will need to be particularly clear about the structure of your argument, so that your assessor is not confused by the presentation of conflicting evidence. Some key tactics in making sure your argument is clear include:

- framing a very clear main contention (your response to the topic)
- selecting appropriate quotations and textual evidence
- constructing your paragraphs carefully, remembering to use linking sentences to create flow and a cohesive argument.

For the topic above, a key contention might be 'the text shows that family relationships can be perfect until they are ruined by traumatic events'. Another possibility is 'this collection shows that despite good intentions, there is no such thing as a perfect family relationship' – this is the contention underlying the sample response paragraphs and notes below. Remember, there is no 'right' or 'wrong' contention, but you must be able to support it with evidence from the text.

Sample introduction

> Representations of family life are central to many stories in Cate Kennedy's collection *Like a House on Fire*. While characters often show evidence of having genuine compassion for each other, the reality in most stories is that family dynamics are fraught with conflict, misunderstanding and disconnection. Often, external factors – ranging from illness and injury to work pressures or financial struggles – influence individuals' equilibrium, in turn placing stress on interpersonal relationships. Few stories offer evidence to contradict this reality, and thus the collection as a whole suggests that there is no such thing as a perfect family relationship.

Body paragraph outline

Paragraph 1 – Identify examples of key family relationships in the text, specifically noting *how* these relationships are imperfect.

You might group these by type, such as:

- families whose members don't share values and therefore experience disconnection (for example in 'Flexion', 'Ashes', 'Five-Dollar Family', 'Whirlpool')
- families in which external pressures have damaged otherwise positive relationships (for example in 'Like a House on Fire', 'Cake', 'Static', 'Seventy-Two Derwents').

Paragraphs 2–3 – Expand the assertion in the previous paragraph, providing more depth and using specific quotations to support your argument about *how* relationships fall short (and how Kennedy shows this).

- Past events (the miscarriage) underlie current tensions in 'Flexion'. Kennedy often describes Frank's body language to illustrate the discomfort in the relationship (Frank is 'crablike', moves 'suspiciously' and 'grunts', p.10).
- In 'Whirlpool' there is direct conflict (shown in direct dialogue) as well as distancing (shown in the father's symbolic absence in past photos, and the fact that he barely speaks).
- The repetition of 'humiliation' throughout 'Like a House on Fire' and the central imagery of a house on fire highlight the deterioration of the family dynamic with the protagonist's injury.
- In 'Static', Kennedy uses contrasts to show the pervasive conflict throughout the extended family, including the contrasting financial states of Anthony's and his sister's family; the contrast between Anthony's and his mother's gifts for Tom, or the contrast between past and present Marie.

Paragraph 4 – Acknowledge contradictory evidence, i.e. family relationships that appear to be flawless, then counteract this evidence in order to support your overall contention.

- In 'Tender', Christine is close to Al and they share ideals and beliefs; they both also love the children.
- However, she still refrains from discussing her fears about her diagnosis, keeping her emotions from her family and instead suffering alone.
- In 'Seventy-Two Derwents', the relationship between Tyler and her sister Ellie is presented as idealistic: supportive and positive.
- However, this is the exception in a very unhealthy dynamic where there is conflict between the adults in the house, and the mother fails (until the very end) to support her children adequately.

Sample conclusion

While there are positive family relationships in a few of Kennedy's stories, the stories are still embedded in problematic family situations, emphasising the unattainability of perfection in any family dynamic. They illustrate many possible causes for the imperfections in interactions, ranging from internal, personal reasons such as conflicting values, to external influences such as the impact of tragedy or illness, which is a strong theme throughout. As a whole, the collection shows that, even when people have good intentions, they are unable to maintain perfect family relationships.

SAMPLE ANSWER

'The characters in these stories are all finding ways of "keeping up appearances".' Discuss.

Characters in Cate Kennedy's *Like a House on Fire* exert considerable effort to maintain a facade of respectability and strength that belies their personal sorrows and desperations. They are often portrayed as disingenuous and out of touch with reality, yet the collection does not endorse giving up entirely, as those who do not bother to maintain outward appearances are not rewarded with positive outcomes. Thus the collection presents a complex view of the value of keeping up appearances.

The point of maintaining facades, in this collection, is to convince either outsiders or oneself that reality is better than it actually is. In 'Ashes', it is a secondary character – Chris' mother – who illustrates this. She has a particular way of keeping up appearances – mainly for her own benefit, it seems, and particularly about past events and memories: 'to give them a patina of something richer and happier'. Chris believes his mother has 'embroidered ... the truth ... under stiff layers of decorative restitching' and finds it hurtful that she wilfully ignores aspects of the past, such as the nature of her relationship with his father. We are encouraged to accept Chris' view that this 'nauseating ... revisionism' is an unhealthy way of experiencing the world; Kennedy facilitates this by presenting the story from Chris' first-person perspective.

Other stories similarly examine how individuals' refusal to accept an unpolished reality damages others around them. For example, the mother in 'Whirlpool' insists on capturing a perfect family photograph for her overseas acquaintances, creating an idealised version of her family, although in reality, its members do not get on well. The photography session is miserable – particularly for the protagonist Anna, who is already suffering at the hands of a mother who refuses to accept the reality that her daughter is growing up. Instead, she forces Anna to wear a childish sundress, clinging to a version of the truth that suits her own feelings. Again, Kennedy ensures that we side with Anna, critiquing the integrity of the photography session in which the effort of playing happy families is characterised by Anna's 'dead, robot smile' and the fact that the family members are, physically, unnaturally close together.

The photography in 'Whirlpool' is a motif echoed in other stories. It represents keeping up appearances – either for others, as in 'Whirlpool' and the end of 'White Spirit'; or for themselves, as in the Christmas photo in 'Static' and in 'Five-Dollar Family', where new mother Michelle makes a huge physical effort to have a family photograph taken, knowing it will be her only opportunity to capture an image of the family she wishes she had.

The motif also extends to other forms of imagery. For example, art is a form of escapism for Tyler in 'Seventy-Two Derwents', and with the diorama in 'Tender' Christine builds an image of a world simpler and more positive than the one in which she lives, filled as it is with uncertainty, fear and physical vulnerability. The diorama she creates is 'golden afternoon sun pouring over an Enid Blyton countryside. Magic hour', a representation of the reality she would like. Similarly, at the heart of 'White Spirit' is a mural that purports to represent the multicultural estate; in actuality it presents an outsider's idea of the estate, one recognised by the minister – an outsider – as sending a 'positive message' even while residents are 'distancing themselves, with subtle and infinite dignity'. The mural is a time- and money-consuming enterprise that has little value to those for whom it allegedly speaks.

While such false realities are portrayed as unhelpful and even hurtful, Kennedy's stories also critique characters. For example, Rebecca in 'Cross-Country' illustrates the extremes of what can happen when individuals cease attempting to keep up external appearances. Rebecca has taken so much time off work she no longer cares about it; she has become disconnected from her friends; she is no longer eating well or looking after herself, but rather lies 'heavy as a stone' in bed, putting all her energy into unproductive and ultimately pointless online stalking. Ray in 'Sleepers' is similarly unsuccessful, living in a friend's shed and failing to move on after his break-up. When presented in contrast with the other stories, the fates of these seemingly hopeless characters suggest that, while denial of true reality is problematic, there are worthwhile reasons for upholding an idealised version of one's life, rather than surrendering to despair.

The notion of keeping up appearances is central to *Like a House on Fire*. It is closely linked to the theme of maintaining hope; Kennedy shows that life will always throw up challenges, but what is most important is to maintain hope. Without it, there is little likelihood of emerging from difficult times. In presenting idealised versions of themselves to the world – whether through images or through their own beliefs – characters in these stories embody what is admittedly sometimes a clumsy and hurtful hope. While not all the characters in the collection attempt to do this, those who do not are shown to be failing in their own lives, suggesting that maintaining face is an important skill.

REFERENCES & READING

Text

Kennedy, Cate 2012, *Like a House on Fire*, Scribe, Victoria.

Reviews and interviews

Ley, James 2012, 'Home fires too close for comfort', *The Australian*, 13 October, http://www.theaustralian.com.au/arts/review/home-fires-too-close-for-comfort/news-story/68f5c33bf7c400c06b5688e3c1a1057c

Mills, Jennifer 2013, 'Domestic fiction', *Overland*, 13 March, https://overland.org.au/2013/03/domestic-fiction/

Watts, Madeleine 2013, 'Interview with Cate Kennedy' in *Griffith Review Edition 42: Once Upon a Time in Oz*, Griffith University, https://griffithreview.com/articles/interview-with-cate-kennedy/

White, Jessica 2013, 'Review of *Like a House on Fire*', Jessica White's personal blog, 15 April, http://www.jessicawhite.com.au/ladyredjess/2015/3/25/review-of-like-a-house-on-fire

Other websites

Steele Rudd Award Judges 2013, 'Judges' report extract', 8 September, Scribe Publications, https://scribepublications.com.au/news-events/news/like-a-house-on-fire-wins-the-steele-rudd-award

Stella Prize Judges 2013, '*Like a House on Fire* Judges' report', http://thestellaprize.com.au/prize/2013-prize/like-house-fire/